D0031214

THE
LONELY GUY'S
BOOK OF LIFE

ALSO BY BRUCE JAY FRIEDMAN

Novels
STERN
A MOTHER'S KISSES
THE DICK
ABOUT HARRY TOWNS

Short Story Collections
FAR FROM THE CITY OF CLASS
BLACK ANGELS

Plays
STEAMBATH
SCUBA DUBA

THE LONELY GUY'S BOOK OF LIFE

Bruce Jay Friedman

McGRAW-HILL BOOK COMPANY
New York · St. Louis · San Francisco
Toronto · Mexico · Düsseldorf

1 2 3 4 5 6 7 8 9 0 B P B P 7 8 3 2 1 0 9 8

Portions of this book have appeared in somewhat different form
in the following publications: *Esquire, New York* and *Signature.*

LIBRARY OF CONGRESS CATALOGING IN PUBLICATION DATA
Friedman, Bruce Jay, date
   The lonely guy's book of life.

   1. Single men—Anecdotes, facetiae, satire, etc.
I. Title.
PS3556.R5L6   818'.5'407   78–16958
ISBN 0–07–022432–3

Book design by Barbara Hall

To BJF
This one's for you, fella.

CONTENTS

INTRODUCTION
WHO ARE THE LONELY GUYS?

Who are the Lonely Guys?

They tend to be a little bald and look as if they have been badly shaken up in a bus accident. Jules Feiffer obviously had "Lonely Guy" stamped on his forehead in the cradle. Buck Henry. Guys like that. But it gets tricky. Woody Allen is doubtful. We're not talking shy here. That's another book. The Shy Guy's book. Warren Beatty gets you mixed up because of all his dating. He may be a secret Lonely Guy. Why else would he have made *Shampoo*, which winds up with him on a hill, albeit a Beverly Hill, puzzling over the folly of the human condition? Jack Nicholson's too quirky. You might not want him on the team, but John Ehrlichman seems to be a Lonely Guy, especially when he is gathering literary materials down there in New Mexico. John Mitchell, too. A Conservative Lonely Guy.

Except for Truman, all presidents are Lonely Guys since they have to go off regularly and make decisions that affect the hearts and minds of all Americans for generations to come. They usually do that after lunch. One blooper, and that's it, for an entire generation to come. All of which makes for a tense Oval Office Lonely Guy. Was Nixon a Lonely Guy? Even at the crest of his powers, he ate a lot of Lonely Guy food. American cheese sandwiches and pale vanilla shakes. Until he started drinking those wines. Yet even his wines were Lonely Guy San Clemente wines.

Network heads are visionary Lonely Guys and so are the fellows in charge of FBI district branches. There are very few gay Lonely Guys unless you want to count some British ones who turn up at the seaside. It's possible there are entire gay couples that are Lonely Guys. Women can be Lonely Guys, too. Female stand-up comics, for example. Also women who are sensitive but are trapped inside lovely faces and bodies. Certain Wilhelmina models are in this pickle. She's not going to be throwing any eggs in the pan at four in the morning, but Jacqueline Onassis may be a Lonely Guy. On nights when she has been escorted to the ballet by the wrong Iranian. Kierkegaard was probably the first Modern Day Lonely Guy, although he may have disqualified himself when he came up with faith. (Lonely Guys know what the score is in this department.) Howard Hughes went over the line when he let those fingernails grow. Right fielders are Lonely Guys. So are free safeties, doormen and large dogs. Horses are Lonely

Guys unless they are the spoiled favorites of girls named Wendy in Darien. All of Canada may be a Lonely Guy. "Boat People" thought they were Lonely Guys until they got settled in suburban homes in Sacramento. Married people are fond of saying that they are Lonely Guys, too. But this is like marching in solidarity for Choctaw rights, when you're not a Choctaw. No Polish directors are Lonely Guys since any time they like they can just reach out and grab a script girl and some caviar.

Lonely Guys lean against railings a lot and stare off in the distance with bunched-up jaw muscles. They had a bad time at summer camp and are afraid they are going to be sent back there, even at age forty. From the street, they peer in at cocktail lounges, through the potted palms, and decide the place is not for them. They take naps in the early evening and are delighted to wake up and find it's too late to go anywhere. A favorite activity of the Lonely Guy is to take a walk down by the river. Lonely Guys start to fill out forms with great enthusiasm, then quickly lose heart, right around the part that asks for their mother's maiden name.

This book is written not in celebration of the Lonely Guy, since obviously there is not much to celebrate. But it is designed to let him know that someone is aware he is out there. And that he is not alone. There are millions like him, even though he has only a small chance of meeting the attractive ones. The Lonely Guy may decide that he doesn't *need* a book, but this is entirely beside the point. If he is going to co-exist with his fellow Americans, he has got to learn to accept gracefully things he doesn't want.

The book may be picked up and read at any old place; the chapters do not follow in any rigid sequence, and in that sense, the book is like the Lonely Guy's life, one phase of it relentlessly like the next. Care has been taken to address the specific problems of the Lonely Guy—such as what to do with little left-over pieces of soap. On occasion, the reader will be led to the door of wisdom, only to be asked to wait outside for a while. The perceptive Lonely Guy will see that this approach, too, is a deliberate one, designed to mirror the quality of the life that awaits him. Never mind that it would have been much more work to write a book that actually delivers the goods.

Does life itself deliver the goods for today's Lonely Guy?

This book, finally, is your companion, Lonely Guy, a loyal comrade in the battle against a world you never made—and one that often seems to wish you would go away.

Read around in it, clutch it to your thin chest, and do not leave it on someone's buffet table.

BJF
Penn Station, 1978

PART ONE
THE BASICS

BRIEF BIO OF A LONELY GUY

• He married a woman because she smelled like gardenias. She also did a perfect imitation of Cyd Charisse.

• They chose the suburban town in which they wanted to live because it had an attractively rustic name.

• They named their child after a bit player in a late-night movie.

• He picked his divorce lawyer because the fellow had an office in Madison Square Garden where the Knicks, Rangers and all his favorite teams played.

THE LONELY GUY'S APARTMENT

THE LONELY GUY'S APARTMENT

At college, he was quite shy with women. His ap-
proach was to say "Hi there," tell the woman his
name and then say: "Some day I would like to have
an apartment overlooking New York City's East
River." He could not recall one instance in which a
woman responded to this technique.

A Lonely Guy's best friend is his apartment. Granted,
there is no way for him to put his arms around it,
chuck it under the chin and take it to a Mets' game.
But it is very often all he has to come home to.
Under no circumstances should he have an apart-
ment that he feels is out to get him. One that's a
little superior. An Oscar Wilde of an apartment. No
Junior Studio will ever throw its arms around the
Lonely Guy and say: "It's gonna be all right, babe."
But it should at least be on his team. Perhaps not

a partner on life's highway, but somewhere in his corner.

If you are a brand-new Lonely Guy, the chances are you have just been thrown out and have wound up draped over the end of somebody's couch. Either that or you have booked a room in an apartment-hotel for older folks who have Missed Out on Life. There will be a restaurant in this kind of hotel where people take a long time deciding if they should have the sole. You don't want to become one of those fellows. As soon as you get movement back in your legs, try to get your own place.

Many Lonely Guys will settle for a grim little one-roomer in which all they have to do is lie there —everything being in snatching distance of the bed —contact lens wetting solution, Ritz crackers, toothpicks, Valium, cotton balls, etc. This is a mistake. No Lonely Guy can thrive in an apartment that comes to an abrupt ending the second he walks through the door. There is no reason why he should have to go to the zoo for a change of scenery. Or stand in the closet. The Lonely Guy in a one-roomer will soon find himself tapping out messages to the next-door neighbors or clutching at the window guards and shouting: "No prison bars can hold me." It's important to have that second room even if it's a little bit of a thing and you have to crawl into it.

The best way to smoke out an apartment is to check with your friends. Everyone will know someone who has seven months to go on a lease and wants to sublet. Someone who's had a series shot out from under him. But this may not be the best way to go. Living in an apartment with seven months remaining on the lease is like always waiting for the toast to come up. Try to get one with a decent amount of time remaining, eighteen months or two years, so you can at least feel it's worth it to get your Monterey Jazz Festival posters on the wall.

Rental agents can be useful, except that they tend only to handle apartments with wood-burning fireplaces. If you say you don't want one, you get marked down as an uncharming fellow who didn't go to acceptable schools. The tendency of the new Lonely Guy will be to grab the first place that looks better than a Borneo Death Cell, just so he can get off the street. He doesn't want to make a career of looking at vacant apartments which still have other people's old noodles in the sink. It will be worth your while to hold out, to contain your retching just a few days longer and ask yourself these questions about any apartment before you snap it up:

How Is It for Taking Naps? Lonely Guys take a tremendous number of naps. They are an important weapon in the fight to kill off weekends. Before renting an apartment, make sure it has good nap potential. You might even want to borrow the keys from the rental agent, lie down and test-nap it.

7

What Would It Be Like to Have Bronchitis In? Bronchitis, that scourge of the Lonely Guy. Call up any Lonely Guy you know and he's likely to be in the last stages of it. (Lonely Guys don't wash their vegetables.) But it's an excellent test: Is this the kind of place I'd want to have Bronchitis in or would I feel ridiculous?

What About Noise? Tomb-like silence is not always the ticket. It can be dangerous for a Lonely Guy to sit around listening to his own pulse. Some noises aren't bad. The sound of an eminent chest specialist with a persistent hacking cough can be amusing. But make sure there isn't a lady above you named *Haughty Felice* whose specialty is chaining up stockbrokers and hurling them into play dungeons.

"Get in there, Dwight, and start worshipping my stiletto heels."

Nothing is more unsettling than to hear a commodities expert rattling his handcuffs at four in the morning.

Do I Want This Apartment Waiting for Me When I Get Back from San Francisco? The Lonely Guy may often be sent to San Francisco to whip a sluggish branch office into shape. When he returns, there will never be anyone waiting at the terminal to hail his arrival. This is always a clutch situation. The well-traveled Lonely Guy deals with it by holding back his tears and impatiently shouldering his way through the crowd, pretending he's got to catch a connecting flight to Madrid. Still and all, if he gets out of the airport at one in the morning, and there isn't a wonderful apartment waiting for him, all warmed up and ready to go, that could be it, right there, ring-a-ding-ding, into the toilet for good.

Is It Over-Priced? The Lonely Guy has been taught two things, ever since he was a little tiny Lonely Guy: (1) Never kneel down to inhale bus exhaust fumes. (2) Keep the rent down.

It's time to take another look at that second one. All terrific apartments are over-priced. The only ones with low rents are downwind of French restaurants that didn't get any stars at all in dining-out guides.

When it comes to rent, it's probably best to cut down on other things, like molar insurance, and pay through the nose, if that's what it takes to get a winner. On the other hand, don't pay so much rent that you have to live on *Milk Duds*. Or that you're always mad at your apartment. Remember, it's not the apartment's fault that it's expensive. There is nothing the apartment can do about it. Can it help it if it's great?

Is This Apartment Really Me? That's the Big One. Freud told his followers that when it came to making major decisions they should listen to their "deep currents." You might find an apartment that would be

9

just right for the early struggling Gore Vidal. Or for Harry Reasoner right now. But does it have *your* name on it? Listen to your deep apartment currents on this one. Ferenczi, a disciple of Freud's, listened to his and admittedly committed suicide. But not before he'd enjoyed many happy months in a charming little duplex in Vienna.

In sum, you need a great apartment.

There will be times when it will be just You and Your Apartment against the World.

Get yourself a stand-up apartment.

Here are some more apartment insights:

ONE GREAT FEATURE

Before you sign the lease, make sure the apartment has at least one special feature—a natural brick wall, a sunken living room, smoked mirrors—so that when you are walking around aimlessly, you can stop suddenly and say: "Jesus, look at those smoked mirrors. And they're all mine, until the lease is up." That one terrific feature might even be a dignitary. Then you can go around saying: "I've got a little place in the same building as John Travolta's dermatologist."

TERRACE TIPS

The Lonely Guy with a decent income should try to get himself a terrace. The most important thing about a terrace is to make sure it's screwed on tight.

A lot of them fall off and are never reported because people are too embarrassed, the way they used to be about rapes.

Along with the terrace, it's essential to get a Monkey Deflector. Many big-city buildings have South American diplomats living in them who keep monkeys that will swing in at you. Chileans are especially guilty of this practice. They will insist the monkeys are harmless—"Just give Toto a little yogurt"—but if you check with the doorman, you will find out they are biters.

Once you have a terrace, don't feel obliged to throw over your adult life to the care of potted flowers. Toss a few pieces of broken statuary out there and tell visitors: "I'm letting it go wild." This will impress women who have been raised in Sun Belt trailer courts.

THE JOY OF LIGHTING

Too much emphasis cannot be placed on the importance of good lighting. The Lonely Guy with an uncontrollable urge to bang his head on the refrigerator may be reacting to sallow, unattractive light. Lighting should be warm and cozy and there should not be too much of it. An excess will remind you that there isn't anyone wonderful in there with you. Too little will have you tapping along the walls to get to the bathroom. A sure sign that the lighting is wrong is if you spend a lot of time taking strolls through the building lobby.

Unfortunately, there is no way to tear off a piece of lighting you like and bring it down to the lighting fixture people. There is no such thing as a swatch of lighting. One kind not to duplicate is the harsh, gynecological type favored by elderly Japanese civil service officials who like to spy on their sleeping nieces.

Lighting fixtures are tricky. Some will give off a cool and elegant glow in the store, and then turn around and make your place look like a massage parlor. The best way to get the lighting right is to experiment and be prepared to go through half a dozen lamps to get the right one. It's that important. Some of the finest light is given off by the new Luxo lamps. Unfortunately, they look like baby pterodactyls, and Lonely Guys who've used them complain that their lamps are out to get them. A great kind of lighting to have is the kind they have at a bar you love in San Francisco. Shoot for that kind.

VIEWS

The worst view you can have is a bridge, particularly a *Lost Horizon* type that's obscured in fog at the far end. In no time at all, the Lonely Guy will start thinking of it as a metaphor for his life, stretching off into nowhere. Some other things not to have as a view are prisons, consolidated laundries and medical institutes. The Pacific is not so hot either unless you're into vastness. Interiors of courtyards are tolerable, but will tend to make you feel you should be writing a proletariat novel or at least in some way be clawing your way to the top. The world's most unnerving view is when you can see just a little bit of a movie marquee; the only way to tell what's playing is to stretch all the way out the window while another Lonely Guy holds your ankles. The most relaxing view is the Botswana Embassy.

PEOPLE WHO CAN HELP YOU DECORATE

The Last People Who Lived in the Apartment. When you move in, don't rearrange anything that was left behind. Chances are the previous tenant knew more about decorating than you do. He may even have been a tasteful Lonely Guy.

The Moving Men. Many have good decorating instincts, especially if they are out-of-work actors. A danger is that they will make your apartment look like an *Uncle Vanya* set. But if your own decorating instincts are shaky, leave things exactly where the moving men set them down.

Any Woman Who Worked on a Major Film. Invite one over, don't say a thing and have a normal evening. At some point, reflexively, she will move a sconce or something several inches and you will see a boring room explode with loveliness.

The Woman at the Department Store. Every department store has a handsome woman in her fifties who is assigned to help Lonely Guys. She will have a large bosom, generous haunches and will set you to thinking about Dickensian sex with your mother's best friend in front of a hearth. There is no need to seek her out. She will spot you at the door of the furniture department. (There is some evidence that she is in league with the divorce courts and that you may have been phoned in to her.) Work with this woman, though cautiously. No matter what your sensibility, she will see you as a craggy, seafaring type out of a late-night movie ("Dash my buttons if you aren't a handsome-looking sea-calf") and pick your furniture accordingly. Upon delivery, many of her choices will not fit through your front door. Why does she pick out furniture that's too big to fit in? No one knows. She earns no commissions on this massive stuff that has to go back to the store. It may have something to do with her ample haunches. Get her to try again by coming on smaller.

FEAR OF DECORATORS

Many people are terrified of decorators, afraid they're going to be given widely publicized Bad Taste Awards if they don't go along with every one of the decorator's recommendations. It's because of those "to the trade only" signs on all the good furniture stores. Just once, talk back to a decorator. The experience can be exhilarating.

> DECORATOR (a woman with orange hair): I've thought it over and you're getting Riviera Blinds for your living room.
> LONELY GUY: No, I'm not.
> DECORATOR (astonished): What?
> LONELY GUY: You heard me. I hate Riviera Blinds. And I'm beginning to hate you, too.
> DECORATOR: How about the track lighting I ordered?
> LONELY GUY: Hate it. Send it back.
> DECORATOR (after a pause): You're right on both counts. I'll get rid of the 'verticals,' too.
> LONELY GUY: The 'verticals' stay. I've always had rather a fondness for 'verticals.'
> DECORATOR (with new respect): You're hard to work for ... but *so* challenging.

A WORD OF CAUTION ON DESKS

The easiest thing to buy is a desk. Rough-hewn ones made of driftwood, rolltop desks, elegant French ones upon which the first acts of farces were written. The Lonely Guy must be careful not to buy a whole bunch of them; if he does, his apartment will soon look like the city room of a scrappy small-city daily.

ASHTRAYS

It's important to have a lot of ashtrays around and not just to accommodate smokers. When they cook, most Lonely Guys have nothing to bring the vegetables out in. Certain ashtrays can pass as a charming new kind of vegetable platter. The peas, for example, look just great in a big bright ashtray.

BOOKSHELVES

Books give an apartment a scholarly pipe-smoking look. Many rock-oriented young women will assume you wrote all the books in your shelves—that you were once named Coleridge. Don't over-do it and turn your place into a library. The saddest book story is that of Lonely Gal Eleanor Barry (reprinted in its entirety from *The New York Times,* December 21, 1977).

> A 70-year-old woman was pulled out from under a giant pile of books, newspapers and press clippings that had collapsed on her, but she died shortly after being rescued. The pile fell on Eleanor Barry as she lay in her bedroom, and according to police in Huntington Station, Long Island, the weight of the papers muffled her cries for help. She died Sunday.
>
> The police said they had to use an axe to smash the door of the bedroom because the collapsed pile blocked their entry. They said that the house was filled with towers of books, newspapers, shopping bags and assorted papers.

THE ENDS OF THINGS

It's important to put some focus on the ends of things as the Lonely Guy will be spending a great deal of time huddled over there in a corner. An investment in a bunch of good strong end tables, for example, will not be wasted. It's important, incidentally, to keep couches manageable in size and not have them stretching off in the distance. What's the point of being the only fellow on a long freight train of a couch! Other, juicier opportunities for loneliness and isolation will be coming your way. And stay away from Conversation Pits. The Lonely Guy who's rigged one up will quickly see that he is the only one on hand to sound off on America's lack of a clear-cut natural gas policy.

A TRICKY DECISION

Do you go with overhead mirrors? There is no question that they are fiercely erotic, especially if you can talk an *au pair* girl into slipping under one with you. But what about those nights when you're just a poignant guy staring up at his own hips! The makers of overhead mirrors are conservative and confidence-inspiring, many of them respected Italian-Americans with no connections to the Gambino family. But they cannot absolutely guarantee that an overhead won't come down in the middle of the night and turn you into a whole bunch of Lonely Guys. For this reason, it might be wise to pass.

17

PLANTS

Buy a lot of them. Scattered about, they will cover up the fact that you don't have enough furniture and aren't knowledgeable about room dividers. A drawback is that each day you will see little buds and shoots, life perpetuating itself while yours may very well not be. Buy your plants on the opposite side of town. They are always cheaper over there. Refer to your plants as "Guys." Put your arm around one and say: "This guy here is my avocado."

ROOM FRESHENER

Lonely Guy apartments tend to get a bit stale, so it's important to load up on room fresheners. The way to apply one is to hold it aloft, press the aerosol button and then streak through the rooms as though you are heralding the start of the new Olympics. Some of the fumes will flash back and freshen *you* up, along with the apartment. Many a woman who has admired a Lonely Guy's cologne is unwittingly in love with his room freshener.

A SHEET AND BLANKET PROGRAM

One kind of sheet to be wary of is the elastic bottom one that curls over the four corners of the bed and supposedly stays there. As soon as you buy them, they no longer fit. The biggest problem is that they tend to break loose in the night and snap you up in them.

Silky, satiny sheets feel good to the skin and will give you an inkling of what it's like to be Bob Guccione. But what you get is a combination of sleeping and ice-skating and there is always the danger of being squirted out of bed. Just buy colorful sheets you like.

The time to change sheets is when you can no longer ignore the Grielle and Zweiback crumbs in them.

Salesmen will tell you that East German llama blankets are the warmest in the world and are so tightly woven that the thinnest shaft of cold can't sneak in there and get at you. None of this is important. The only way to test a blanket is to hold it up to your cheek and see if it feels fluffy. (The sight of this is heart-breaking and will help you in picking up saleswomen.) Better to have ten fluffies than one llama that holds off chilly weather but has a hostile Cold War feel to it.

SHOWER CURTAIN MADNESS

The trick in getting a shower curtain is to find one that fits right. Shower curtains are either long, flowing things that look like gowns worn by transvestite members of the Austro-Hungarian General Staff, or else they are shorties that will remind you of Midwestern insurance men whose pants don't come down far enough. Bob Dole fans.

There is the possibility that the Lonely Guy is incapable of buying any shower curtain at all. And that he will have to wait till Ms. Right comes along. If such is the case, and you plan to go without a shower curtain, the trick is to let the water hit your chest so that as much of it as possible bankshots back into the tub and doesn't rot your tiles. If enough of it gets out there, you will run the risk of plunging through the floor to the Lonely Guy below.

SILVER SEPARATORS

Lonely Guys with mangled hands are usually assumed to be veterans of Iwo. This is not necessarily the case. Too often, it's a result of reaching into kitchen drawers to try to get knives and forks out. The way around this is to buy a silver separator that has little rows for utensils. On the other hand, many Lonely Guys would rather sever an occasional artery than stand around filing butter knives.*

PICTURES YOU ARE NOT SURE OF

Lonely Guys have a tendency to accumulate paintings they are not quite sure of—gifts from dissident Haitians or suburban women who've suddenly left their families and moved into Soho lofts. The way to

---

* Another way to deal with silverware is to slap it up in full view on a magnetic wallboard. However, the underweight Lonely Guy with a metal watchband runs the risk of being sucked right up on it, along with the knives.

deal with such a painting is to prop it up on a dresser and put stuff in front of it—a clock, a Fundador bottle, a book about the fall of the once-proud Zulu nation—so that only some of the painting shows through. Make it look as if it's ready to be hung, but that you haven't gotten around to it. (You don't know where the nails are anyway.) That way, if someone admires it, she can push aside the obstructions and say, "Hey, watcha got there, fella?" If she hates it, you're covered because you've put all that stuff in front of it, indicating you don't think it's so hot either.

THE RIGHT AIR CONDITIONER
Get a strong, no-nonsense air conditioner that sends the cold air right up the middle at you. A Larry Csonka of an air conditioner. Don't get one in which the air wanders out in a vague and poetical manner so that you have to run around trying to trace it.

THE RIGHT TV SET
The most important thing about a TV set is to get it back against something and not out in the middle of a room where it's like a somber fellow making electronic judgments on you. Odd-shaped TV sets make a lot of sense; a tall skinny sliver of a TV set can actually spruce up a dying sitcom. But don't make the mistake of getting a lot of little tiny sets and scattering them about like leftover snacks. Get

one solid-looking Big Guy that you can really dig into.

The prospect of a little TV-viewing section with some throw pillows strewn about and a prominent bowl of shelled walnuts may be dismaying to the urbane Lonely Guy—but its effects are likely to be calming.

GAY CLEANING FELLOWS

Now that you've got your apartment, who's going to clean it up? Good news in this department. Now that *Chorus Line* is a smash and has spawned international companies, there are a lot of dancers who couldn't get into any of them and have become gay cleaning guys. They aren't that easy to find. It isn't as if they advertise conspicuously under names like Joan Crawford Clean-Up and play selections from *Gypsy* on their answering services. They are usually under an Italian name like Fuccione and Calabrese.

Yet such a macho-sounding company can send over a bright-eyed and cheery gay guy with a handkerchief on his head. The best thing about gay cleaning fellows is that they are not afraid of ovens. They go right after them, all the way to the back end, sponging up the last droplet of lambchop grease. Gay cleaning fellows also know all about the latest cleaning stuff: you may have to take a little ribbing about not having Lemon Pledge Dusting Wax for your breakfront. On the plus side, though, they are considerate enough to Leave the Windex to You, the only fun part in all of cleaning. The only gay cleaning fellows to be wary of are ones from East Germany who may try to Cross That Line. Unless you don't mind waking up on a Sunday morning to a gay cleaning fellow named Wolfgang who has already started on *The New York Times* Art and Leisure Section.

CLEANING FOR POVERTY-STRICKEN LONELY GUYS

Some Lonely Guys are needy,* and have to clean up their own apartments. If that's your situation, wait till just before company comes and then get down on your knees and roll up all the dust in the room in a big ball. Most of it will come right up, but stubborn dust that refuses to can be dabbed off the floor with a damp palm. Lonely Guys who live around Phoenix and have a sassy Jack Nicholson style may elect to get into dustball fights with another Lonely Guy.

THE BIG PICTURE

As a general rule, don't buy anything for your apartment that you can't take along with you. When you batter down a wall to give it an ecclesiastical grotto effect, you may be supplying a free ecclesiastical grotto effect to the next Lonely Guy. Only the strict-

---

* The state of being in a Negative Cash Flow Situation.

est interpretation of Maimonides (a biblical Lonely Guy) requires you to do so. The last thing you want to do is put down roots. At a moment's notice, you should be ready and available to pull up stakes and try your luck at being a Lonely Guy in St. Paul de Vence.

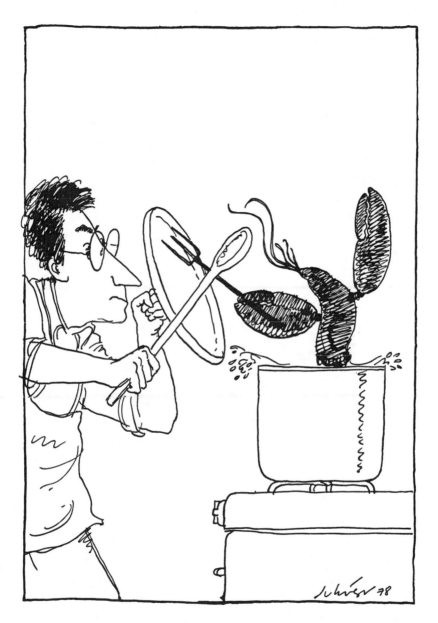

THE LONELY GUY'S COOKBOOK

THE LONELY GUY'S COOKBOOK

He did not like summer camp as a five-year-old and was embarrassed because he had a hunch-backed counselor. One day, he ate some turnips and became deathly ill. His mother arrived, concerned, compassionate. When she saw how sick he was, she took him home to recuperate. But as soon as he recovered, she sent him right back to the camp with a note, saying, "Here he is again. And he is not to be given any more turnips."

Everyone knows that eggs are the basic Lonely Guy's food. Four in the morning, all alone, throw on some eggs, delicious. But what happens when eggs have lost their charm? When one plate of sunnysides blends unhappily into the next? What happens when the Lonely Guy is egged out?

This is a cookbook for the Lonely Guy who is ready to move Beyond Eggs.

There won't be any braising in this cookbook. Lonely Guys would rather fight than braise. Nor will you be called upon to julienne or mince. In the darkest of all circumstances, there may be a little dicing, but that's about it. No dredging, no rendering. The Lonely Guy is in no position to put in long hours rendering fat.

What you will find is a modest game plan for nourishment which the Lonely Guy must think about if he has some tattered idea of surviving. Several general approaches to cooking will be suggested, along with a few ideas for dishes that will stick to your ribs. Follow these simple procedures and stick to your ribs they will.

MEASURING THINGS

Forget about measuring things. Just tear off hunks of things and toss them in. Lonely Guys are too upset to be dealing with 1½ tsps. of nutmeg which they won't have around anyway.

DIET, CHOLESTEROL, THAT STUFF

Forget about diet, cholesterol, that stuff. As a Lonely Guy, you deserve only delicious things, even when they are on the fat side. You need all the strength you can get. And remember that *no diet anything tastes good*. Have you tried the new skinny sodas? *Yccchhh!* So get only fat sodas, raspberry and black cherry, the ones you forgot about. They keep them over in the corner. As a Lonely Guy, you will be aggravated a lot and this in itself will tend to keep your weight down. (There will be mornings when you wake up with a sinking feeling and won't want to eat anything at all. That's good for shearing off a few pounds a month right there.)

Eat only incontestably wonderful things—salami, whipped butter. Better to Be a Fat Lonely Guy Than Never to etc., etc. But don't overdo it. Nobody Loves a Dead Fat Lonely Guy. So that you don't become one of those, try to eat a skinny thing every time you eat a fat one. Follow up pizza with a radish. After fried chicken, take a few swallows of grapefruit juice. The fat thing clogs up your arteries and the skinny thing opens them right up for traffic. They've got studies on that. You will practically be able to feel the fat and skinny things fighting it out inside your body.

DARING IN THE KITCHEN

Don't be too daring in the kitchen. For example, don't suddenly get involved with shallots. Later, when you are no longer a Lonely Guy, you can do shallots. Not now. If you know coriander, stay with coriander and don't fool around. Even with coriander you're on thin ice, but at least you've got a shot because it's familiar. Stay with safe things, like pepper.

HOW WOMEN CAN HELP

Get a cooking tip from every woman you either have an affair with or have been married to. Every woman has one such terrific tip. A single bay leaf in liver and onions. Putting not only salt but sugar, too, in the vegetables before you cook them. That may be all you got out of a ten-year-marriage—putting sugar in the vegetables—but it's something. A pinch of curry in the salad dressing—these tips start to add up, especially if you fool around a lot. And each tip will remind you of the old affair. Every time you sprinkle Tabasco sauce on a sardine sandwich, it will bring back Karen Feinschreiber.

SHORTENING

Forget about shortening. Nobody really knows what it is.

LEFTOVERS

Somewhere along the line, you will meet a school-teacher who will tell you to wrap up your leftovers in Baggies.* What a treat it will be to come across them a few days later when you least expect it. This is not true. What you will come across are little piles

---

* Baggies can also be used for getting your shoes into your galoshes. Stick a Baggie on, and the shoe will slide right in. But that's it for the Baggie. Don't forget yourself and wrap a ham sandwich in a Baggie that's been used for galoshes. Unless you're sure it's been turned inside out.

of old coleslaw which are taking on lives of their own. So when you've had enough to eat, *throw everything out.* Dumping half a western omelet will lift your spirits. You may be a Lonely Guy, but the last thing you want to be is an Unclassy Lonely Guy.

VEAL

Veal is the quintessential Lonely Guy meat. There is something pale and lonely about it, especially if it doesn't have any veins. It's so wan and Kierkegaardian. You just know it's not going to hurt you. So eat a lot of veal.

Veal is gentle and benign and can be used in combination with any number of items—peppers, sausages, tomatoes, etc. But veal has its limits. Don't push veal. Don't mix it in with peppermints, for example, and expect to come up with much.

THE BIG THREE

Start every dinner by sautéing onions, peppers and mushrooms in Filippo Berio olive oil. Nothing tastes bad if it starts off with those three. You can then proceed with fish, or chicken—it's not important. Or say you're dashing back and forth between the kitchen and *The Bionic Woman,* trying to decide if Lindsay Wagner has tits. You might just decide to wolf down the onions, peppers and mushrooms and go with Wagner.

THE PHILOSOPHY OF CHICKEN

You will be working a lot with chicken. The main thing about chicken is the size. Many supermarkets sell giant wings and breasts that scare the hell out of you. They seem to have been hacked off a chicken on the run. A case for L. A. coroner Thomas Noguchi. So get smaller pieces, although not *too* small because then you're into a whole dwarf freak-out. You can also buy clean pressed-down slabs of white-meat chicken, although these seem to have been bought in an office-supply store and bear little relation to the crazy barnyard animals you once knew and loved.

ADDITIONAL CHICKEN INSIGHTS

Before you fry chicken, take the skin off. Lonely Guys don't realize you're allowed to do that. They think there's some agreement that the skin stays with the chicken right down to the wire. You're allowed to rip it right off. It doesn't hurt the chicken either. The chicken is way past that. If you're cooking the chicken in the oven, pour some honey on it. This tastes delicious and does not make you a gay Lonely Guy.

A SHOCKER OF A TIP

Don't be too quick to throw in the towel on burned stuff. Some burned stuff tastes great. Burned French toast, burned string beans, if you remembered to put a lot of butter on them. This does not mean burned through and through, big-time burned. If it's cremated, get rid of it. We are discussing burned where there is still some good stuff left. Burned around the edges but not in the middle. If it's major-league burned, remember to throw out the pot, too, because the last thing you want to be is a Lonely Guy using Brillo.

A MAN ON BASE

Buy things that are already cooked and almost delicious. This will give you a Culinary Man on Base. All you have to do is come in and hit a long fly ball. Don't, for example, do spaghetti sauce from the gun. If you do, you might as well have married that Pier Angeli look-alike you found in the ruins of Sicily while you were with the Occupying Army. Then you would really be a Lonely Guy because you would have grown and she wouldn't have. Buy an *existing* spaghetti sauce—they keep them bland for old folks—and start heaving things in. Onions, cucumbers, garlic—anything improves spaghetti sauce unless it's something freaky like melon balls. (You can even throw in melon balls if you're in certain areas north of San Francisco.)

OTHER ITEMS TO BUY THAT WILL GIVE YOU A MAN ON BASE

• Cooked lobster, served cold. All you have to throw on is lemon and cocktail sauce.

• Bean soup. You hardly have to throw anything in except maybe hot dogs. You can throw in lentil soup, too.

• Potato pirogen. Throw on any spice you can get your hands on.

A BASIC LONELY GUY BREAKFAST

A bagel, strawberries and coffee prepared in a Mr. Coffee machine. Where are the eggs? You've had your Lonely Guy eggs at four in the morning with Sinatra music. You've had a sort of pre-breakfast. And you don't want to do any cooking till later on. The bagel will have a nice crispy wake-up taste to it. The strawberries are almost ridiculously healthy. This breakfast will tend to make you think of Chaim Potok and Beverly Hills, but eat it every day. Once in a while you can eat nectarines instead of strawberries. But do not make any substitutions for the bagel.

TABLE SETTINGS

Grit your teeth and set the table for one, no matter how excruciating and lonely a process this is. Otherwise you will have a tendency to eat the whole thing while you're crouched over the sink. Another thing to grit your teeth and do is clean up quickly, perhaps after you've had your first bite. If you wake up the next day and see an old half-eaten salmon croquette, it's liable to push you Beyond Loneliness into Forget-About-It City, a place where you don't want to be. Make sure to throw out beer cans, unless you live in the back of a diner, in which case they will fit in with the decor. After a while, a girl named Alma will come and take them away.

A custom at dinner parties is for the host to Present the Table, gather all the guests around the Buffet and introduce each dish. "This is the *saumon fumé*, this is the *Escargots à la Provençale*." As a goof, and to cut through the gloom, try Presenting the Table to yourself one night. Stand alongside your supper and say aloud: "This is the salami, this is the mustard, this is the rye bread, this is the cherry soda." Then give yourself a brief round of applause and, after a big guffaw, sit down and dig in.

FROZEN MILKY WAYS

Keep a handful in the freezer. You'd be surprised at all the times you're going to want one. Only watch yourself, because Loneliness loosens teeth. There may be studies on that.

A BASIC LONELY GUY LUNCH

Turkey leg, a pickle and cream soda. You can eat this every day, too, only make sure not to take any phone calls because you will grease up the receiver.

SMELL EVERYTHING

This is important because certain food-store operators may spot you as a Lonely Guy and use you to try to lay off a marginal slice of flounder.

Things are usually done when they smell good. Wait for the good smell, then pounce on it and start your eating. This almost always works.

REFRIGERATOR TIPS

Try to have a refrigerator with more than one shelf in it. Otherwise everything will soon get all lumped together like in a duffel bag; at the end of the year, you'll find a lot of boxes of fish sticks and wonder what to do with them.

LIVER

The best thing about liver is how virtuous it makes you feel after you've eaten some. People won't admit it, but they feel that somehow it connects onto their own liver. There are no studies to support this. Eat some anyway. If you are cooking some bacon, you can make a last-minute decision to throw a few slices of liver in the pan. The bacon will kill the taste of the liver, and this will get rid of your liver-eating obligation for some time.

SALAD DRESSING

Every supermarket has a terrific Italian woman who lives nearby, bottles her own salad dressing and sells a few dozen to the supermarket. You'll find them near the okra. These are great because the Italian woman has not gotten cocky yet. As a result, her stuff is thick and full of garlic. She has to try harder, etc. Once Angela gets franchised it will be all over.

THE MYTH OF THE CAESAR SALAD

Caesar salad is a salad that has been made to seem complicated but isn't. They say you need romaine lettuce, but you don't. Any lettuce will do. You want to go with a crunchier lettuce, go with it. Then it's oil, vinegar, a raw egg, cheese, anchovies, lemon juice, garlic, you know the type of thing. *And big croutons*. That's the key. Little ones crumble up and feel like the beach at Easthampton. On the other hand, don't use giant croutons. The Crouton That Took over St. Louis. Then you'll be eating a giant crouton with little dribbly gardens of Caesar salad hanging off it; there's no need to do that.

CRAB BOIL

Sounds like the worst thing ever invented. Smell it, though, and you'll see that it's slightly fascinating. Figure out something to throw it on. Shrimp is a possibility. A car engine. Anything. Keep crab boil in the back of your mind.

EQUIPMENT
- A lot of giant frying pans.
- A chopper. Try to get one that doesn't make you

spend all your time digging the chopped stuff off the chopper.

• Terrific-looking knives. Easier said than done. Salesladies will refuse to sell a Lonely Guy the knives he wants, claiming that the coating will come off in the dishwasher. Only skinny, terrible-looking knives will keep their coating. *Don't fall for this.* Insist on the terrific-looking ones. Even when the coating washes off, they look better than the ones that keep their coating. If you live in a densely populated urban center, you'll be able to slip a few of your knives into your coat pocket when you have to run downstairs for things you've forgotten.

• A lot of sponges for grape-juice stains. Lonely Guys spill a lot of grape juice.

GARLIC

One of the great treats about being a Lonely Guy is you can use all the garlic you like since "who cares?" Use it on everything except Rice Krispies and melon balls. Just for the fun of it, run into a delicatessen and holler out the French name for garlic: *Aiiieee.*

A treat for garlic-lovers is Slow-Cooked Garlic Chicken. This is not a dish in which the chicken is cooked in a slothful and heavy-footed manner. It means dousing the chicken with garlic and cooking it for a long time, an hour and a half or so, at a temperature of 280 degrees. In that manner, the garlic

will penetrate to every part of the chicken, under
the arms, the feet, everywhere. No part of that
chicken is safe from this garlic onslaught which is
what you've always wanted in your dreams.

POUNDING

The butcher does this. Some people think it means
putting their meat into tidy one-pound packages. It
doesn't. It means taking the fight out of it. Don't let
your butcher do it. As a Lonely Guy, the last thing
you need to see is meat that's been beaten into
submission and lost its will to survive.

MEATBALLS

Unless you've got a lot of time on your hands, there
is no way to keep meatballs round and bouncy.*
Eggs won't do it. Neither will bread crumbs. Only
compounds developed in the space program have a
chance of keeping meatballs round. So be prepared
to have them go to pieces on you. As a Lonely Guy,
it may not be pleasant for you to see a meatball go
to pieces. Take comfort in the fact that even meatballs that have come apart at the seams can be
reasonably delicious.

---

* One suggested method is to slip them into the freezer,
half an hour before cooking. Unless your timing is exquisite,
and you snatch them out of there just in time, you'll wind
up with little meatsicles that have no real function.

A BASIC DINNER: LONELY GUY VEAL PARMIGIANA À LA TOMATE

Quickly eat some lettuce with Roquefort dressing. Your salad will be out of the way and you won't have to worry about it.

Have a drink. Stolichnaya Vodka with Clamato. It's all right to keep Stolichnaya Vodka in the freezer because of its low freezing point. And if they are wrong and it freezes, hack off a piece and drink it when it thaws out. If you are in a hurry, suck it.

Take the veal out of the wrapper, the veal that you haven't allowed the butcher to pound into submission. Put it where you can find it, against a dark background, since it's pale and will tend to disappear on you.

Have your second Stolichnaya Vodka with Clamato.

Get the Big Three going in Berio olive oil. Put it in your biggest frying pan.

Try to find the veal. If you come up with it, squoosh it around in a mixture of eggs and crumbled-up corn flakes. Hold on tight and make sure it doesn't slip out of your hands. Otherwise, you will lose it down the drain. A lot of great veal has been lost that way. Get the veal going in another big frying pan.

Try to keep your nerves steady, because you are about to do a *third* thing. Only Lonely Guys who have been chopper pilots in Nam will be able to stay calm at this point. Put some existing tomato sauce in a pot and start heaving things in—every spice you can come up with. Remember, though, that bay leaves tend to take over.

Somehow, get all of this together—the veal, the tomato sauce, the Big Three—in one giant frying pan as big as a football field. (Don't get all excited and squirt Right Guard in the pan; Lonely Guys often keep Right Guard in the kitchen.)

Lay strips of mozzarella cheese on the veal. Turn the oven up to four hundred degrees, set the whole creation in the oven and run like a sonofabitch.

Have a glass of wine. You can use some from a leftover bottle. It does not lose its body. That's all a myth designed to get you to buy lots of wine. Leftover wine has a pleasingly sullen taste to it.

Take careful peeks into the oven, making sure to crane your head in another direction so that the oven doesn't explode on you. When the dish looks the way things look in reliable neighborhood Italian restaurants, take it out and plunge in.

To be fair to this dish, it must be eaten when it's hot enough to sear the roof of your mouth.

This recipe can be used with chicken, meatballs or fish, although fish will make it a little boring.

BACK-UP RESTAURANTS

In the middle of cooking, you may suddenly slump over, unable to continue. For this reason, it's good to have some late-night back-up restaurants that serve bacon cheeseburgers and Chinese food. It is important that these restaurants be festive, because when you arrive you're going to be down three touchdowns. They should have at least a handful of women around who are known to be "sure things."

HAVING PEOPLE OVER

The only reason to have someone over is so that she will feel sorry for you when she sees that none of your dishes match. When you bring out your glasses —leftover from three-in-a-carton shrimp cocktails— it will break her heart. Within a week, she will send over a complete set of dishes and a chopper. Be careful, though. She will try to end your Lonely Guy status, which you don't want to do quite yet.

Good luck to you in your life as a reasonably well-fed Lonely Guy.

GROOMING

GROOMING

The father had lived through many great and turbulent events in history—the outbreak of World War One, the Lindbergh Kidnapping. Hitler's March into Poland. Roosevelt's Fourth term, man's first walk on the moon. The Phenomenon that amazed him the most, however, took place each morning when his son would get up, put on his pants, tighten the belt and then try to stuff his shirt in through the belt. He never could get over that.

Who cares how I look, the Lonely Guy will ask. My grocer? Why should I take the trouble to smell nice? Is there a line around the block waiting to smell me? All I ever do is slip around corners. Do I have to be well-groomed to do that? In sum, why should I be a Well-Groomed Lonely Guy?

These are sound questions. And there *is* a case to

45

be made for bad grooming. (You don't have to do anything. You just lie there and vegetate, etc.)

But remember: Good grooming eats away at the clock, that scourge of the Lonely Guy. Taking showers, opening up tight mouthwash bottles, trying to get anchovy paste stains off a shirt—all this can kick the hell out of a day. Before you know it, a week is gone. Ask any Lonely Guy what an advantage that is.

Good grooming can fake people into thinking you are not in agony. This is a good thing. If people ever realized how lousy you felt, they simply would not stand for it, the way they couldn't take Bangladesh. They would break down doors in an effort to rid you of your Loneliness, which, of course, is all you've got going.

With minimal effort, the Lonely Guy can be almost as well-groomed as a normal person. One example should suffice: Many Lonely Guys cut their toenails and don't bother to catch them up in anything. They take no responsibility for them whatever, allowing them to fly all over the place. The Well-Groomed Lonely Guy keeps an ashtray alongside his feet, like a target, and lets the toenails carom off this. A *p-i-n-n-n-g* sound results which is not altogether unpleasant. From this point on, it's a simple matter to collect the toenails and get them the hell out of there. You won't be able to trap every last one. Is anyone saying that you will? But let's say you get eight out of ten. That's eight toenails you won't have to worry about again. Hats off and goodbye. No nightmares about a cute girl's picking up a handful and saying, "What the hell are these?"

THE SMELL OF LONELINESS

Let's face it, Lonely Guys have a smell of their own. You've read about it in novels. "Axel had a smell of loneliness about him." It's not bitter or acrid or anything, but it *is* a little stale, like an old herringbone suit. Nothing much can be done about it. It's socked all the way in there. But the Lonely Guy has a responsibility to himself and to the community to go after that smell. That means taking plenty of showers. Generally speaking, the Lonely Guy should avoid baths. It hardly requires pointing out here that an occasional Lonely Guy, snug and secure in a warm tub, will decide to stay right where he is, packing it in, then and there. Contrarily, there is no known instance of someone deciding to end it all in a shower, by, say, getting up on his toes and smacking his head against the nozzle.

Any sweet-smelling soap will do, though preferably not one that's so slippery you have to keep chasing after it. Some Lonely Guys have reported results from a dab of dishwasher detergent. The most important thing about soap is not to save up a whole bunch of skinny leftover pieces of it. Many an affluent Lonely Guy, who would think nothing of buying a Ferrari, will turn right around and start saving little pieces of soap. Or worse, try to mash them together to make a new bar out of them. When it gets around three-quarters of the way down, throw the soap away and accept your loss graciously. Each time you start a new bar, you will experience a clean Born Again feeling.

While any soap will do, that's not quite the case with shampoos. One of the biggest mistakes a Lonely Guy can ever make is to buy a tar shampoo. Admittedly, it will make his hair smell fresh and outdoorsy. But it may also make him feel he is wandering around in the woods somewhere, lonelier than ever. Worse, it might conjure up thoughts of fall, the hardest of all seasons for the Lonely Guy to get through, each falling leaf a stake in his heart. (Summer, when everyone else is going away, isn't so wonderful for him either. Neither, for that matter, is winter, when the whole world is out there playing with Snowmobiles and he isn't. The best time for the Lonely Guy seems to be a two-week span at the end of March when not much is going on.)

Before leaving the shower, feel around and make sure to pull out the hairs that get caught in the drain. No one is saying you have to do this after every single shower. But don't make the mistake of many Lonely Guys and let it pile up so that it has to be trucked out of there.

Make sure your towels are not only fluffy but

large. What's the point of having a towel if it will only dry one knee? You'd be surprised at all the Lonely Guys who will use thirteen tiny little towels for a single shower. So use a big towel, but not one that's so huge you feel lost and abandoned in it. Some Lonely Guys like to warm up their towels, like dinner rolls. This is all right, so long as you don't drape them over a toaster. They can be heated up on a radiator or even put in the oven, but don't get carried away and throw a grilled cheese sandwich in there, too.

Just because a towel is a little dirty in one place is no reason it has to be rushed over to the laundry. There may be other places where it's still a little clean. Lots of other places. When these are used up, it *still* doesn't have to go to the laundry. A cute girl can be invited over to take a shower and to use the suspect towel. When she's gone, the towel will smell fresh and pretty again; you will be amazed and delighted to see how many showers it has left in it.

Talcum powder is excellent for after-shower grooming so long as you don't snort or swallow it. There is no known antidote for swallowed talcum powder. The Lonely Guy who has it in him will have to resign himself to a life with powdered internal organs.

In selecting a deodorant, the Lonely Guy should pass up the roll-on type and go after the spray variety. The reason for this is that the Lonely Guy usually forgets about the deodorant until his shirt is on. It's much easier to spray right through the shirt than it is to try to get the roll-on up through the sleeve until it makes contact with the armpit. And don't be afraid to spray a little underarm deodorant someplace else, on your feet, for example. This is not an arrestable offense. "All right, men ... put the cuffs on him. Guess where he put underarm deodorant. ..."

Many Lonely Guys who were bearded through the social upheaval of the Sixties have now returned to shaving, only to run into that same old puzzle— how to deal with the Adam's Apple. Most Lonely Guys have a prominent one, as a result of having to gulp down so much bad news. The Adam's Apple is the most delicate part of a man's body. For this reason, it makes no sense to keep nipping off the end of it. Lonely Guys with responsible dads learned early in the game that there is only one way to go at an Adam's Apple: Pinch the skin out, swing it to one side, shave, then swing it back the other way, and shave again. Simple enough. But how many Lonely Guys have reached the age of forty and have been in the dark about this technique? How many, to this day, wear turtlenecks to cover up a hairy Adam's Apple?

To stop the flow of blood caused by shaving gashes, many Lonely Guys use little dabs of toilet paper which they stick on there. The main drawback is that they often forget to take them off and have to be pulled aside at parties and told about them. Short of a strangulating tourniquet, the best way to stop up a shaving gash remains the styptic pencil, one of the few constants in American life. It is the only item in Western civilization to have undergone no technological breakthrough. During the long years of early space exploration, many of us here on the ground wondered how it would benefit the styptic pencil. The answer, sad to say, is that it didn't.

The Lonely Guy who has finished up shaving will be well advised to check his nose hairs and consider trimming them back. Not after every shave. Not even once a week, necessarily. But at some point. Does it make any sense to wait till you're tripping over them? No. A sign posted in the foyer saying "Trim Back Nose Hairs" may offend a guest or two but will serve as a reminder of this important grooming step.

BRIEF FASHION ANALYSIS FOR THE LONELY GUY

It isn't important that the Lonely Guy plan his outfits days in advance or slave over the coordination of his colors. But it's nice for him to have a "look." This can be pulled off with a single identifying trademark—a peaked cap, a maroon windbreaker, or even an old college T-shirt that he wears—rain or shine.

The clothes-conscious Lonely Guy may also want to have a suit made for special occasions. This will require many trips to the tailor so that his measurements can be established on grid lines and properly hooked up to a satellite. Then, the Lonely Guy can order suits from anywhere on the globe and have the fun of saying:

"Hi, I'm Tom Henderson. Get out my grid lines. I'd like to order a suit; I'm calling from here in Damascus."

It's a waste of money to have shirts made to order —except for the measurement that gives you room enough to slide your watch *under* the cuff—so you don't have to jam your cuff under the watchband.

ORAL HINTS

To insure excellent breath, a good mouthwash is recommended. The Lonely Guy with Dragon Mouth is not going to get very far in life. One way to tell if your mouthwash is too strong is to see if you can still taste liverwurst. However, some Lonely Guys have given up mouthwash and gone over to liverwurst. Up in the morning, mouth a little stale, cut a slice of liverwurst, wash it down with Clamato and you're in business.

An amazing number of Lonely Guys go through their lives in terrible fear of swallowing toothpaste. This is ridiculous. What kind of life is that! It *could* put you out of business, but you would have to wolf down tube after tube of it and who's going to take the time to do that? So pick out a more reasonable fear, for heaven's sake.

COLOGNE AGAIN, NATURALLY

It's essential that the Lonely Guy select just the right cologne. Sounds easy, but it's hard to tell what a cologne is like if you're the one it's on. Many Lonely Guys choose their cologne on the basis of the bottle.

"That's quite a bottle. These cologne guys must know something about cologne."

Another way to look at it is if they've spent all that money on a great bottle, there was probably no money left for the cologne. Or they're using a wonderful bottle to pass off a crappy cologne. But this is the Conspiracy approach to American life again, coming back to haunt us, and it should probably be kept out of colognes. Think in between. Choose a nice-looking bottle.* But don't insist that it be carved out of stained glass by Dominican friars.

One way to check out a cologne is to put some on, walk out of the room and then dash back in and smell the place you were. Another is the time-honored Elevator Test. Apply the cologne and step into a crowded elevator at noontime. If the other passengers huddle in a corner and begin to swat the air in front of them, you may be on the wrong track. If they shift from one foot to the other, but steadily hold their ground, you are probably in the clear.

Once you've selected a cologne, stick to it. Don't

---

* Some of the best colognes are the ones in frosted bottles at the barber shop. (They look like Gilbey's gin bottles.) But you've actually got to *be* a barber to own one of those.

put one cologne on your face and another on your feet, totally confusing the person who is smelling you. And stay away from colognes that are too macho and make you want to kick everyone in the stomach.

BEYOND THE SHOWER

The Lonely Guy must not only keep himself clean but also look after the clothing that he wears. His best friend in this department is Woolite, which can get any item in the world Slightly Clean. This product has virtually put dry cleaners out of business. When shown a container of Woolite, many have been known to punch out at it. To use Woolite, put your dirty clothes in a sinkful of cold water, sprinkle some in and let everything soak for around three minutes. It's that cold water that gets people suspicious. How can you get stuff clean with cold water! Everyone's a little shaky on the answer, but what seems to happen is that the dirt gets cold. And cold dirt doesn't seem to smell as bad as hot dirt. Something like that. In any case, it's important to make your return to the sink in three minutes. Clothes left overnight in Woolite tend to rot away when you're wearing them at parties. Don't worry about getting all the Woolite squeezed out of the clothing. Woolite itself has a nice smell and can be used as an emergency cologne. Now, only every six months or so will you have to take your clothing to the laundry. Lonely Guys have been known to buy cabins in

Vermont with the money they saved on Woolite. They become lonelier than ever once they do that— but that's another story.

Quite often the Lonely Guy will have a favorite leather jacket that doesn't smell so hot after a while. No amount of Woolite can get through to it. For this situation, there is a special process called Deep Steam-Cleaning which penetrates right through to the DNA structure of the jacket and makes it sweet-smelling again. This process costs as much as a Toyota, but it is worth it to the Lonely Guy who only feels secure in that one favorite jacket.

Buttons, too, are best left for the dry-cleaner. No Lonely Guy should ever attempt to sew one on. When he tries and fails to thread the needle, he will be reminded of the erosion of his capacities, his decline and eventual you-know-what. Once the first button has fallen off something, it's safe to assume that all the others will follow. Sewing them back on one at a time is like trying to shore up the Thieu Regime. When the first one goes, cut bait and take them over to the dry-cleaner; he will machine-sew them on so that they will still be standing there—like the British Empire—long after the shirt has fallen apart.

THE CHINESE LAUNDRY

A word about Chinese laundries. Isn't it time we took a hard look at them? After all these years, they still insist they didn't put starch in your collar—

even if you crack off a piece of collar and eat it right on the spot. Quietly they've sneaked up the prices which are now on a par with Gold Coast Cleaners, right down the block. Many a Lonely Guy has gotten into financial hot water by going on expensive vacations, thinking he's saved all that money by using Chinese laundries—when he hasn't saved a dime.

If one of your shirts comes back with a sleeve gone, suddenly all they know how to talk is Chinese. Worst of all is that skinny string they put on bundles which gives you finger and palm gashes. Many feel that this is their way of undermining the Western democracies—but this is probably going too far. Don't feel you are smoothing over Chinese-American relations by continuing to use their laundries. Leave that kind of thing to Secretary of State Vance.

Be firm with your Chinese laundry. Maybe if we all become Chinese laundry hard-liners, we can get them to give out free litchi nuts again.

A TRIO OF GROOMING TIPS

Shoe Polish. Many Lonely Guys let their shoes get dirty because they're afraid to get polish on their cuffs. This is absurd. Polish on the cuffs can actually be an advantage, serving as a fashion segue to your shoes. Something new in color coordination. On the other hand, getting polish on the hands is a legitimate fear since it must be removed surgically.

Food stains. Almost every Lonely Guy makes the mistake of trying to get food stains off, which of course, usually makes the problem worse. Say you're dealing with marinara sauce on a shirt. Moisten the towel, dab it on the trouble-spot and slowly rub the towel around in an ever-broadening circle so that the entire shirt is covered with a light marinara sauce hue. This is better than having just one conspicuous marinara sauce spot.

Putting Things Away. On occasion, the Lonely Guy will wake up with a sinking feeling that's worse than the one he usually has. He can't figure out what's wrong with him. The answer may be a simple one. He has a lot of old gray T-shirts lying around. Nothing is more depressing than seeing this. For a feeling of well-being, put things away. Stick your dirty socks in a drawer with the clean ones; it's not important. You'll worry about this later. The main thing is to get them out of sight.

In sum, try to look and smell as nice as possible. Remember, the clean, well-groomed Lonely Guy is a Lonely Guy better able to face the future, no matter how peculiar that future may be.

LONELY GUY
ON THE RUN

LONELY GUY
ON THE RUN

His best sport was tennis. He had a slashing, almost mystical forehand. At a Midwestern college, he took on all comers, defeating All-American types named Bryce and Jamie. After a year of this, he laid down his racket and never played again. He felt certain that a legend would spring up about a slender mysterious boy from the East who almost magically pulverized everyone in sight and then disappeared. But no legend sprung up. He kept checking, but as far as he knew, no one ever mentioned him again.

One of your main problems as a Lonely Guy is energy. Not President Carter's kind. The other kind. Where on earth are you going to get some? One answer is running. Even if you have to drag yourself out there to do it, you'll wind up healthier than you were.

Running is basically a Lonely Guy activity. If you

61

doubt it, go out and run and start waving to people running toward you and see what happens. No one will wave back. The only ones to respond at all will be people who are curious about everything that moves.

As a runner, you've got to go it alone.

WHAT IT DOES FOR YOUR BODY

One of the wonderful things about running is what it does for your body. Your belly will gradually get whittled down until it's small and hard and round. Unfortunately, it won't go away completely, but will remain in the form of a hard little volleyball of a belly. Running will also give you sloping shoulders and a thin haunted appearance which is irresistible to Finns. Don't be surprised if you develop a high adenoidal whine, like someone who was tortured in Algeria.

Some of the fat that gets pared down may tend to collect in the form of high, billowing steatopygic buttocks, common to Zulu warriors. Make sure you're not one of the fellows that happens to.

TOUGH FEET

Make sure you have tough feet. Practice on little piles of gravel. Distance running has been called a tribute to the indomitable human spirit when actually it's a tribute to human feet. Many people don't make it in running because their feet are quitters. They are willing to go on, but their feet always want to throw in the towel. All the great Marathon runners* had wonderful feet. If you could shine a flashlight on Frank Shorter's** feet at midnight, you'd see that he has better ones than anyone else, that he actually has unfair feet and in a sense runs a spitter.

WHAT TO WEAR

The proper outfit for running is a department store track suit with a single stripe on it so that cars don't crash into you. These outfits are inching up in price. Some of them cost more than real suits and are nice enough to wear to discotheques. Don't get an overfancy running suit that's covered with fluorescent stripes, though, or you'll look like a roadblock.

If you wear shorts, make sure they are trim and not the bouffant type. Don't wear shorts at all if you have white hairy legs. (Don't run around *naked*. Just cover up those legs.)

A jockstrap is recommended so long as you don't keep snapping it in irritation when you're not having a good run. See that your socks are even in height or you will make the runner in back of you seasick.

---

* Every runner dreams of entering the Boston Marathon but doesn't do it for fear of coming in last. "And now, in position number 6000 ... Mr. George Kreevy." So what if you're last! Look at Phil Jackson. Nobody's first choice for the NBA Hall of Fame. Yet nothing wrong with him.

** U.S. Gold Medal winner for Marathon, 1972.

It's all right if your socks are a little gray. Knowledgeable runners know that gray socks are not necessarily filthy and might even be a little clean by Lonely Guy standards. Wear sneakers that are comfortable, even if they are for another sport. It's not an arrestable offense to run in squash sneakers. They don't immediately pull you over. All that stuff about special sneakers for punchball, or special rowing sneakers, was started by the sneaker bigwigs so that a person would be embarrassed if he didn't own at least forty pairs.

It's offensive to run while fully dressed, wearing business shoes and socks that have little clocks on them. Don't be one of those guys.

ON YOUR WAY TO RUNNING

Lonely Guys who live in the city will have to run past stores and buildings to get to wherever it is they're going to do their running. Along the way, doormen and supermarket checkout guys will needle you by running along with you for a while. Just ignore them and take it in a good-natured way. Otherwise, they will stay with you, and there's nothing more embarrassing than to run for miles with a supermarket checkout guy matching you stride for stride.

When you're standing on the corner in your shorts, waiting for the light to change, don't shift your weight from one foot to another or you'll be arrested as a hooker.

A PHILOSOPHY OF RUNNING

It's terribly important to develop a Philosophy of Running. What you've got to do is eliminate all feelings of competitiveness and just run for the feeling of health and well-being. Since this is impossible, the next best thing is Beating Guys. This is not as easy as it sounds. There are not that many guys around you can beat. Fat Guys are misleading since a lot of them have piston-like power in their haunches. Catholic High School Guys are out of the question. No one can catch those driven Kennedy look-alikes. And you can forget about fellows from Eastern Europe since every last one of them can run like a sonofabitch. Even Czech film-makers who take a lot of quaaludes are fast runners. Is there any need to get into Orientals? Occasionally, you can beat a Young Guy who is just out there a few times out of guilt from Singles' Bar attendance. You can always beat a bartender.

Once you see that you can beat a guy, you might as well beat him twice and get that the hell out of the way once and for all. The way to do that is to pass him, then slow down as if you're out of gas. When he passes you, start running full out again and Beat Him a Second Time. That will really crush his spirit and you should have no trouble with him in the future. When you've passed him that second time, it's excessive to raise your arms victoriously and sing "Feelin' Free Now" from *Rocky*.

ACTUAL RUNNING

When you're actually out there running, the proper technique is to lift your feet just far enough off the ground so that no one can accuse you of walking. Bouncing along vigorously on your toes looks good but is death on your arches and should only be used to impress girls. Or to spring out of the wings for an *Annie* audition. Don't throw punches at the sky or someone will walk up and start fighting with you.

Take little tiny breaths and make sure no air gets into your lungs, especially if you are running in the city. In fact, do as little breathing as possible. If you have to do a lot of breathing, wait till you get home. Do you want your lungs to look like an old Chevrolet?

GETTING IT OVER WITH

For all of its attractive features, running does tend to get a little boring. So one of your main objectives is how to get the damned thing over with as fast as possible. Along these lines, don't pay any attention to how far you're going or how long it takes you to get there. Otherwise you'll be all caught up in mathematical computations. Just run toward something,

an old lady who sits in the same place every day.*
When you reach her, there is no reason to sit down
with her and get involved with her life. Just turn
around, or tap her if you have to, and start back the
other way. If she is not there, do not panic and go
looking for her in the neighborhood. She'll be all
right.

One way to make the time pass quickly is to lose
yourself in thoughts of space and eternity and the
nature of the universe. This is usually more boring
than running. Another thing to do is write a musical
comedy in your head. This will make you run faster
since you'll want to get back and see how it shapes up
on paper. Still another time-killing device is to make
up Academy Award acceptance speeches.

THE DANGERS

Running is a lot more dangerous than you think.
People assume it's easy and as a result they're not
careful and they fall down a lot. Sometimes they
trip over people who are lying around in the park. It
may not look it, but it's a long way down, especially
if you're a tall guy. The ground is not as close as it
was when you were a kid. Once you see you're going
to fall, go into a roll, taking the blow on your neck,

---

* Many of these old folks have their slacks rolled up so
that their knees can get sunned. Can sunned knees be the
long sought-after key to longevity?

or someplace like that, spring lightly to your feet and try to make it to a hospital. If you think you've broken something, don't move, just lie there in a heap and hope that another runner will drag you out of sight.

Another danger is guys throwing things down at your head from overpasses. Don't run after them unless you're sure you want to catch them.

CHICKEN-WALKERS

Sooner or later, you'll come across a fellow doing an odd and embarrassing strut that is neither running nor walking but some dreadful hybrid of the two. This is the infamous chicken-walker, the loneliest and most despised man in all of sports. So named because of his barnyard gait and the pecking movements of his head. He'll be followed by a pack of kids yelling "Chicken-walker, chicken-walker." Don't assume that you're automatically going to turn into one of these fellows some day. There is no reason why you have to. If you'd like, you can go into a corner where no one can see you, and try a little chicken-walking, just to get it out of your system.

AFTER IT'S OVER

After you've stopped running, don't just stop dead on a dime. Stop gradually, going into a little trot, the way racehorses do. But stop eventually. A lot of fellows like to show off their running by running all over the place, dashing out of stationery stores, challenging cars to races. No one likes that kind of fellow.

When you reach your building after a run, you've got to decide how to get up to your apartment. Do you take the stairs or the elevator? Remember, you're soaking wet and even if it's a healthy animal kind of thing, nobody cares. All they know about is sweat.

If you choose the elevator, there is a strong chance that some woman from New Hampshire will order you off. Your best bet is to ask the freight elevator man if you can go up with some umbrella stands.

Once you're home, don't spoil the whole run by drinking everything in sight. The most you should drink is a couple of bottles of cream soda.

Sometime after you run, you'll probably start to get exhausted and want to take a nap. That's all right, but don't be surprised if your sleep is restless. That's because even though you've finished running, your body may not have had its fill and want to get in some more. Be very careful about this, because during the nap your body may just up and run right out of the apartment.

One of the ways to tell that running is good for you is all the people who will try to get you to stop. A fellow with a perfectly good watch will dart out at you and ask you what time it is. A neighbor in the elevator will warn you that unless you can get your pulse down to around twelve beats a minute you're just wasting your time and may even be destroying yourself. Someone else will insist that you stop running and play tennis. Take a good look at him. He's probably got a mean and cranky face from being on the phone all the time trying to line up partners for doubles and from arguing about whether the ball was on the baseline.

These people do not care about you. They just want you to stop running so you won't be healthier than they are.

Nobody really *enjoys* running. After all, you're not crazy. Even on a cool fall day with a nice nip in the air, it isn't *fun*. It's just not a normal human activity, like sleeping. But once you've finished an exhausting run, and they're all exhausting, you can have the thrill of not having to do it for a while.

So get out there and run—to hit back at all those people who'd love it if you stopped, to feel the joy of getting it over with, and to be a fit Lonely Guy.

EATING ALONE
IN RESTAURANTS

EATING ALONE IN RESTAURANTS

Since money was scarce, their pattern was to order dinners for themselves and an "extra plate" for their son, upon which they would deposit dabs of meat and vegetables. When the boy became center on his high school basketball team, he rebelled one night at Caruso's Grill.

"I don't want any more Extra Plates," he said. "I want a dinner of my own."

"You're not ready yet," said his mother. "When the time comes, I'll tell you. And here, take some of my broccoli. I never liked the stuff here anyway."

Hunched over, trying to be as inconspicuous as possible, a solitary diner slips into a midtown Manhattan steakhouse. No sooner does he check his coat than the voice of the headwaiter comes booming across the restaurant.

"Alone again, eh?"

As all eyes are raised, the bartender, with enormous good cheer, chimes in: "That's because they all left him high and dry."

And then, just in case there is a customer in the restaurant who isn't yet aware of his situation, a waiter shouts out from the buffet table: "Well, we'll take care of him anyway, won't we fellas!"

Haw, haw, haw, and a lot of sly winks and pokes in the ribs.

Eating alone in a restaurant is one of the most terrifying experiences in America.

Sniffed at by headwaiters, an object of scorn and amusement to couples, the solitary diner is the un-wanted and unloved child of Restaurant Row. No sooner does he make his appearance than he is whisked out of sight and seated at a thin sliver of a table with barely enough room on it for an hors d'oeuvre. Wedged between busboy stations, a hair's breadth from the men's room, there he sits, feet lodged in a railing as if he were in Pilgrim stocks, wondering where he went wrong in life.

Rather than face this grim scenario, most Lonely Guys would prefer to nibble away at a tuna fish sandwich in the relative safety of their high-rise apartments.

What can be done to ease the pain of this not only starving but silent minority—to make dining alone in restaurants a rewarding experience? Absolutely nothing. But some small strategies *do* exist for making the experience bearable.

BEFORE YOU GET THERE

Once the Lonely Guy has decided to dine alone at a restaurant, a sense of terror and foreboding will begin to build throughout the day. All the more reason for him to get there as quickly as possible so that the experience can soon be forgotten and he can resume his normal life. Clothing should be light and loose-fitting, especially around the neck—on the off chance of a fainting attack during the appetizer. It is best to dress modestly, avoiding both the funeral-director–style suit as well as the bold, eye-arresting costume of the gaucho. A single cocktail should suffice; little sympathy will be given to the Lonely Guy who tumbles in, stewed to the gills. (The fellow who stoops to putting morphine in his toes for courage does not belong in this discussion.) En route to the restaurant, it is best to play down dramatics, such as swinging the arms pluckily and humming the theme from *The Bridge on the River Kwai.*

ONCE YOU ARRIVE

The way your entrance comes off is of critical importance. Do not skulk in, slipping along the walls as if you are carrying some dirty little secret. There is no need, on the other hand, to fling your coat arrogantly at the hatcheck girl, slap the headwaiter across the cheeks with your gloves and demand to be seated immediately. Simply walk in with a brisk rubbing of the hands and approach the headwaiter. When asked how many are in your party, avoid cute responses such as "Jes lil ol' me." Tell him you are a party of one; the Lonely Guy who does not trust his voice can simply lift a finger. Do not launch into a story about how tired you are of taking out fashion models, night after night, and what a pleasure it is going to be to dine alone.

It is best to arrive with no reservation. Asked to set aside a table for one, the restaurant owner will suspect either a prank on the part of an ex-waiter, or a terrorist plot, in which case windows will be boarded up and the kitchen bombswept. An advantage of the "no reservation" approach is that you will appear to have just stepped off the plane from Des Moines, your first night in years away from Marge and the kids.

All eyes will be upon you when you make the promenade to your table. Stay as close as possible to the headwaiter, trying to match him step for step. This will reduce your visibility and fool some diners into thinking you are a member of the staff. If you hear a generalized snickering throughout the restaurant, do not assume automatically that you are being laughed at. The other diners may all have just recalled an amusing moment in a Feydeau farce.

If your table is unsatisfactory, do not demand imperiously that one for eight people be cleared immediately so that you can dine in solitary grandeur. Glance around discreetly and see if there are other possibilities. The ideal table will allow you to keep your back to the wall so that you can see if anyone is laughing at you. Try to get one close to another couple so that if you lean over at a 45-degree angle it will appear that you are a swinging member of their group. Sitting opposite a mirror can be useful; after a drink or two, you will begin to feel that there are a few of you.

Once you have been seated, and it becomes clear to the staff that you are alone, there will follow The Single Most Heartbreaking Moment in Dining Out Alone—when the second setting is whisked away and yours is spread out a bit to make the table look busier. This will be done with great ceremony by the waiter—angered in advance at being tipped for only one dinner. At this point, you may be tempted to smack your forehead against the table and curse the fates that brought you to this desolate position in life. A wiser course is to grit your teeth, order a drink and use this opportunity to make contact with other Lonely Guys sprinkled about the room. A menu or a leafy stalk of celery can be used as a shield for peering out at them. Do not expect a hearty greeting or a cry of "huzzah" from these frightened and browbeaten people. Too much excitement may cause them to slump over, curtains. Smile gently and be content if you receive a pale wave of the hand in return. It is unfair to imply that you have come to help them throw off their chains.

When the headwaiter arrives to take your order, do not be bullied into ordering the last of the gazelle haunches unless you really want them. Thrilled to be offered anything at all, many Lonely Guys will say "Get them right out here" and wolf them down. Restaurants take unfair advantage of Lonely Guys, using them to get rid of anything from withered liver to old heels of roast beef. Order anything you like, although it is good to keep to the light and simple in case of a sudden attack of violent stomach cramps.

SOME PROVEN STRATEGIES

Once the meal is under way, a certain pressure will begin to build as couples snuggle together, the women clucking sympathetically in your direction. Warmth and conviviality will pervade the room, none of it encompassing you. At this point, many Lonely Guys will keep their eyes riveted to the restaurant paintings of early Milan or bury themselves in a paperback anthology they have no wish to read.

Here are some ploys designed to confuse other diners and make them feel less sorry for you.

• After each bite of food, lift your head, smack your

lips thoughtfully, swallow and make a notation in a pad. Diners will assume you are a restaurant critic.

• Between courses, pull out a walkie-talkie and whisper a message into it. This will lead everyone to believe you are part of a police stake-out team, about to bust the salad man as an international dope dealer.

• Pretend you are a foreigner. This is done by pointing to items on the menu with an alert smile and saying to the headwaiter: "Is good, no?"

• When the main course arrives, brush the restaurant silverware off the table and pull some of your own out of a breastpocket. People will think you are a wealthy eccentric.

• Keep glancing at the door, and make occasional trips to look out at the street, as if you are waiting for a beautiful woman. Half-way through the meal, shrug in a world-weary manner and begin to eat with gusto. The world is full of women! Why tolerate bad manners! Life is too short.

THE RIGHT WAY

One other course is open to the Lonely Guy, an audacious one, full of perils, but all the more satisfying if you can bring it off. That is to take off your dark glasses, sit erectly, smile broadly at anyone who looks in your direction, wave off inferior wines, and begin to eat with heartiness and enormous confidence. As outrageous as the thought may be—enjoy your own company. Suddenly, titters and sly winks will tail off, the headwaiter's disdain will fade, and friction will build among couples who will turn out to be not as tightly cemented as they appear. The heads of other Lonely Guys will lift with hope as you become the attractive center of the room.

If that doesn't work, you still have your fainting option.

PART TWO
LIFE'S LITTLE CHALLENGES AND DILEMMAS

THE WORST LONELY GUY STORY

After twenty-two years of marriage, a television producer left his family and took temporary lodging in a one-bedroom apartment on the top floor of a highrise building overlooking Hollywood's Sunset Strip. At midnight, his second day away from home, it was time for him to take his eardrops and he realized he had never put them in without help. He stepped outside; normally, a few hookers stood around in the hallway, but this time there were none in sight. He took the elevator downstairs and explained his predicament to the doorman. Suspicious at first, the doorman agreed to put them in. The producer knelt down on the lobby carpeting and put his head in the doorman's lap, one ear tilted upward. This is the tableau that was picked up on the security monitors. Armed guards flew out and demanded to know what was going on. They listened to his explanation, but even after they returned to their stations, he could tell they were not convinced.

THE LONELY GUY
WITH
TEMPERATURE

THE LONELY GUY
WITH
TEMPERATURE

He was the only one of twenty-three boys in his neighborhood who did not become either a doctor, dentist or nurse's aide. One day he met the mother of a childhood friend. She told him of her son's various triumphs as a cardiologist in Louisville, then asked what he was doing.

"Teaching English," he said. "I'm chairman of the department."

"That's the way life is," she said, clutching his arm sympathetically. "You just can't always get what you want out of it."

Illness is a stern test for the Lonely Guy. Most people get subtle warnings before they become ill—feelings of edginess, drift, despair. The Lonely Guy has these feelings all the time, even when he is bursting with health. He must rely on more obvious trouble signs

—such as fainting in lobbies and falling out of chair-lifts.

No comforting hand will be there to pull the Lonely Guy through an illness. At the first sign of fever, he may panic, and be tempted to scribble off a note: "I had temperature. I just couldn't go on," then quietly phase himself out of the game.

Such drastic behavior is uncalled for.

Today's sick Lonely Guy stands almost as good a chance at recovery as anyone else.

THE NEW SICKNESS

Sickness may have changed since the last time the Lonely Guy was ill. In the Old Sickness, the Lonely Guy ran a fever and the family sat around waiting for it to "break." Either it did or it didn't. In the latter case, he was removed from his building and that was the last they ever heard of him. For those lucky Lonely Guys whose fever did break, it was full recovery until the time rolled around for them to get sick again. In the New Sickness, fever breaks almost automatically, bringing the Lonely Guy to the door of health. Unhappily, he rarely makes it through. Responsibility lies squarely at the feet of the New Drugs which are game enough in taking on disease but lack the killer instinct. As a result, a small cadre of germs invariably survives, winded, but dead game and ready to sail back in when conditions are favorable.

In the New Sickness, fewer people drop dead—but everyone is a little bit sick all year round.

GOING WITH YOUR SICKNESS

At the first sign of illness, many Lonely Guys quickly take on excellent habits, wearing sweaters, avoiding drafts, washing their vegetables before they eat them. Some sign on at gyms, while others fly south to "bake out." Once a germ takes hold, however, it is too late for admirable behavior. All the sit-ups in the world won't cure bronchitis. No one ever "baked out" the flu. The effort that goes into a last-minute try for health may bring on An Extra Sickness, which you don't need.

A sensible plan is to lie back and Go with Your Sickness; try to understand it and get as much out of it as possible.

DEALING WITH DOCTORS

Each year, testimonial dinners are held for crusty old doctors who braved the elements, year after year, to visit sick patients. Rare is the word spoken in praise of those valiant sick fellows, many of them dead, who braved the elements to visit doctors who would not come to see them.

Unless you live in a stubborn little community in Northern Minnesota, where people give to the land and the land gives back to them—it is unrealistic to expect your doctor to visit you when you're sick.

87

He'll claim that he is too busy. The truth is he doesn't want to. Why should he fight traffic just to see another desperately ill person. You've seen one, you've seen them all.

Unless you can prove legally that your vital functions are slipping away—howls of agony won't do—you will have to settle for a phone diagnosis. The most important thing for the doctor to know is what color your phlegm is now—so make sure you have this information in advance. Unless it is an offbeat shade, like Sienna, this should tip him off to the nature of your disease. If it is swamp green, don't bother to tell him since it is probably too late to do anything about it, and there is no point in upsetting him. Those who live in large impersonal high-rises—and are not sure of the color—can take a little down to the doorman who in most cases will be happy to check it out.

In a phone diagnosis, it is not important that the doctor grab on to the exact disease you have. The main idea is for him to prescribe a medicine that will give you enough energy to get to his office—so that he does not have to go to your place.

A Further Note on Doctors. Many Lonely Guys are more afraid of their doctors than they are of sickness. Rather than call up and get yelled at, they would rather quietly pack it in. Ask yourself this question: Do I have to psyche myself up to call the doctor, as if he were Jacqueline Onassis? If you do, you've got the wrong man.

Avoid funny doctors and those with a colorful mode of expressing themselves.

Here are some lines you don't need to hear from a doctor:

- You'd better sit down for this one.
- What do you have? Oh, I don't know, what would you like?
- I saw your stomach X-rays. Looks like a goddamned junkyard in there.

TEMPERATURE AS A FRIEND

Many Lonely Guys have a Fear of Temperature. Leave it to them, and they would choose not to have any at all, which is absurd, since everyone needs some. Far from being an enemy, temperature can be a friend, a sharp-eyed scout, warning of unattractive rapids up ahead. Admittedly, temperature can get out of control, going over to the other side. In such cases, it should be fought with every means available, like the Fourth Reich.

A high temperature is not always the result of illness. Sometimes, it's brought on by wearing too many sweaters. Or too much time in a sauna. Many a Lonely Guy will be shocked to see that his temperature is 109, theoretically taking him out of the battle.

A possibility is that he has forgotten to "shake down" the thermometer, the most important thing in temperature. This procedure calls for nimble wrists and great energy, none of which the Lonely Guy has when he is sick. Only small NBA forwards can really shake down a thermometer properly.

Reading a thermometer is mostly luck. There is a split second when the mercury lines up with the proper digit, but unless the sick Lonely Guy is on constant alert, like a radar man in the Aleutians, he will miss it and that will be it for the day. In theory, it should be simple to design a thermometer that says "Your temperature is 102" and throws in your horoscope as well, like a drugstore scale. For reasons known only to them, the powerful thermometer bloc has decided against this.

LONELY GUY CHICKEN SOUP

For years, the chicken has been maligned as an absurd and ridiculous-looking creature. Despite these scurrilous attacks, the chicken good-naturedly continues to sacrifice himself in order to provide mankind with the healthiest of all sick foods—chicken soup. No longer do Jewish women hold the monopoly on its preparation. The gentile woman who is not in too much of a hurry because of her budding career can make a perfectly respectable variety.

If he can muster the strength to crawl* into the

---

* Don't be ashamed to crawl when you're sick. It is not as if you've been brought to your knees by tyranny.

kitchen and lift a chicken into a pot, the sick Lonely Guy can make a decent chicken soup of his own. All he need do is surround the chicken with soup greens, adding a beef bone of the kind that is normally tossed to Golden Retrievers if he wishes. The pot should be filled with water so that it covers the chicken and the chicken cannot see out over it. Salt should be used sparingly. There is plenty of time for overkill later.

Lonely Guy Chicken Soup should never be rushed. Eating soup with a raw chicken sitting in it can set you back irreversibly. On the other hand, do not let it cook until you are already fully recovered and don't need it. A particular problem for the sick Lonely Guy is having to get out of bed every few minutes to skim off the fat. A way around that is to leave it on. This is not to suggest that you eat the soup with the fat on it. That *would* delay your cure. The idea is to let the fat sit there until the soup appears to be cooked; then put the chicken on a plate, and slide the soup into the freezer. (Make sure you are wearing warm clothes during this part of the operation, a ski outfit, ideally.) The fat will congeal into a thick lid, something along the lines of a manhole cover. After half an hour, unless the sick Lonely Guy is at death's door, he should be strong enough to lift, or at least roll the lid off the soup.

SICK READING

Sick reading should be on the bland side. Generally speaking, it is a good idea to avoid Greek tragedy, Aeschylus being the worst of all writers for the bed-ridden Lonely Guy. The adventures of Prometheus, bound to a rock, or hundred-headed Typhoeus, trying to get back at Zeus for burying him in the slime, are not a pathway to brighter spirits. The same is true of works on Industrial Safety in the Po Valley. Stick to simple, wondrous stories. Fairy tales and pirate yarns are ideal, although you may experience a shiver of regret that you are no longer a pre-pubescent Lonely Guy.

BENEFITS OF THE NEW SICKNESS

Many sick Lonely Guys assume that the second they take one step out of bed they have to forfeit all sick privileges. This is not true. In preparing for a sickness, the Lonely Guy with foresight will gather round him—or at least have within crawling distance—all the sick stuff he'll need: cough drops, orange juice, Kleenex, something to throw the old Kleenex in. But once he's an officially sick fellow and sees he's forgotten something, that doesn't mean he has to do without it.

In the New Sickness, you can get out of bed and actually sit on a couch and still be considered a sick fellow. Even if you were to slip into a pair of French slacks and take a walk in the hall, technically speaking, you would still be a sick guy. It isn't being in bed—or your outfit—that determines sick status. It's how lousy you feel. So long as you don't go speeding down the Pacific Coast Highway in an open car, you're covered.

SICK AIR

The sick Lonely Guy needs fresh air but at the same time must avoid drafts, which are instant killers. A way to achieve this goal is to open the window, letting the fresh air in, and at the same time deflecting it with some kind of shield, a punk rock poster, for example. Window air is healthful, but tends to be chilly. Keep the radiator on full, but bear in mind the dangers of an entirely separate illness—Radiator Fever. A way to fend this off is to use a room humidifier which will moisten the dry radiator heat. The danger here is that the humidifier, unless carefully controlled, will turn the air dank and fetid, like unexplored sections of the Amazon. Getting sick air just right requires tremendous energy. The Lonely Guy might be better off just lying there and hoping for the best—or exploring some means of bringing in packages of air.

APRÈS-FLU

A moment will come when the Lonely Guy has been in bed long enough and is ready to leave his sickness behind. Whatever charm the sickness had for him has disappeared. He's taken the last tetracycline pill in his five-day series. Theoretically, he should be ready to plunge back into the drabness of his life. Except that he is still sick. Patience is required at this juncture. There is no point in getting angry and trying to sue somebody. Germs very often are tied to a schedule of their own which does not conform to that of the Lonely Guy. It may be a simple matter of their wanting to stick around a bit longer, like getting in an extra day of skiing at Aspen.

When your sickness is at an end, don't make the mistake of telling everyone about it. The Lonely Guy who announces he's been running 102 degrees all week should not be surprised when pretty girls fail to throw their arms around him. The details of an illness are simply not that fascinating. Few people will be enraptured by stories about post-nasal drip. It isn't as if you've spent a month in Gabon, among the Abongo.

The sick Lonely Guy is often convinced that his business affairs have come to a grinding halt. This makes it difficult for him to lie back and get the maximum benefit from his illness. Once he's recovered, he may find that things ran quite smoothly. Vouchers got signed. Despite his absence at the helm, *Yogurt Magazine* shipped right on schedule. The mature Lonely Guy will not be dismayed by this news. On the contrary, it will sharpen his perspective, confirming his suspicion that his efforts in life follow a certain pattern.

Illness offers the Lonely Guy a chance to strike out in a new direction. Too enfeebled to shave, he will be in an excellent position to try out a new beard. His inability to keep down food will get him off to a running start on a new diet. Illness will give him the chance to lie back and get out of the race, in which he was lagging anyway. Most of all, it will offer him a chance to settle, once and for all, the question that nags at all Lonely Guys—considering the quality of his life, is he better off up and around, or in bed with a numbing fever?

BUSINESS AFFAIRS

BUSINESS AFFAIRS

One summer, he worked as a busboy in a hotel. An obnoxious woman kept him coming and going round the clock. She insisted on extra portions and immaculate service. At the end of the summer, she gave him a pair of one-dollar bills for his trouble. In the style of a young Dominguín, he tossed the money back at her and walked away. But he could not resist looking over his shoulder. He saw her pick up the money and put it in her purse, thoroughly delighted to have it back.

As a Lonely Guy, you probably find the business world sinister and mysterious and wish it would all go away. Having let yourself slide a bit, you are probably willing to let your financial affairs go further down the drain as well. *Don't do that.* Loneliness is expensive. It takes a lot of money to keep it going. You need throw pillows. You've got to have cookies, liverwurst sandwiches. You have to have a TV set to lull you to sleep. What about your ear-drops bill, your bathrobes and your cotton balls?

Whether or not you have the strength for it, you have to enter the Dollar War. As a Lonely Guy, you are in a unique position to do so, since what else do you have to do?

Only by running a tight financial ship can you be lonely with confidence and security.

What follows is a guide to the tricky ins and outs of Lonely Guy Financial Affairs.

LOANS

Getting Money from a Friend. Banks, by tradition, never lend money to people who need it. On the other hand, they are delighted to hand over vast sums to people who haven't the slightest use for it. So normally, you will have to borrow money from a friend. In this type of loan, your only obligation is to call up now and then and explain why you haven't paid it back. If the friend calls *you*, he is being rude. Threaten never to borrow money from him again. (There is no need to follow through on your threat.)

Always ask for twice as much money as you need since even a close friend will automatically cut your request in half. Once in a while you may hit the jackpot and get exactly what you have asked for.

Remember, the friend who loaned you the money has done A Good Thing for you. There is no need to run up to him in a restaurant and throw a drink in his face. Many Lonely Guys get confused on this point. It's not the friend's fault that you needed money and he was generous enough to give it to you. (Although it *is* true he could have gotten it over there a little faster. And shouldn't he have *sensed* that you were broke? He's supposed to be a friend, isn't he?)

Getting Money from a Poor Guy. Another good person to borrow money from is a Poor Guy, a starving relative, ideally. Being a needy fellow, he's learned to squeeze every dime and as a result he has socked away plenty in his day. And don't feel bad about borrowing from him, even though he is starving. You're giving him a chance to feel important, possibly for the first time in his life, and that's not mashed potatoes.

Getting Money Back from a Woman. Be cautious about lending money to a woman. Women are equal in almost every way but lag behind seriously when it comes to paying back money. If you ask to have it back, you'll be called a sexist and, almost as bad, an insensitive swine. So when you lend money to a woman, write it off immediately and hope you get it back some day in That Other Department.

Paying Back Loans. One theory holds that when you borrow money, you should pay it back a little at a time. In short, give your creditor something to let him know you are thinking of him. In the words of a famous New York bookie, "Make sure you don't avoit my eyes." This makes sense so long as you pick the right figure. If you've borrowed $10,000, don't send off a check for $18.50, which will only serve as an irritant.

And it's generally not a good idea to send over something other than money—produce, for example, or a sweater. Stick to money. A bag of stringbeans, however well-meant, will only antagonize your creditor.

Second Loans. Having borrowed money from one person, you'll probably scout around and try to find someone else to borrow from. This is ridiculous. You're much better off going back to the first fellow. He's the one who gave you the money in the first place. That proved he had some. And by this time, he's had time to save up some more. The first guy is your man.

CREDIT CARDS

Getting a Credit Card. If you're a Lonely Guy with a steady job, you should have no trouble getting a credit card. On the other hand, Lonely Guy Nobel Prize Laureates may be in for some rough sledding. The reasoning of the credit card companies is that just because someone's won a Nobel Prize, it doesn't mean he is going to win another one. There is no consistency to it. So why should they take a risk on a person like that? In other words, if you're Saul Bellow and stubbornly refuse to take a job in venetian blinds, you can forget about credit cards.

Using Your Credit Card. The most important thing to find out about a credit card is how long they give you before they run over and grab it back. It's important to have several cards so you can mix up your punches, so to speak. When Diner's Club decides it's time to come after you, you can stop using it and begin to take advantage of American Express.

Pay no attention to stores and restaurants that say they *honor* credit cards. Even if they worship and obey them and throw garlands of roses at their feet, it doesn't do you any good unless they actually *accept* them.

Hookers can be charged to your credit cards, but must be billed through organic honey companies. Remember, your accountant will sternly demand to know why you are spending $6000 a year on organic honey, so develop a little thing for it.

Losing Your Credit Card. A big fear is that you will lose your credit card and the finder will immediately run over and charge a cabin cruiser to your name. This is an unnecessary worry. When the cabin cruiser salesman sees *your* name on the card, he will know it is all a big joke.

Disposing of Your Credit Card. At the end of the year, be careful when you are tearing up your credit card. One of the most insidious wounds you can get is from the edge of an invalidated BankAmericard.

BANKS

The Right Bank for You. The Right Bank for You is one that is far away. If it's too close, you'll be running over there all the time; one way or another you won't have any money left. Also, the closer the bank, the easier it is for it to get at you. Try to come up with a bank that uses phones. When you are in financial hot water, many of them will say, "This guy is fading fast. All we have to do is apply a little pressure and we can bring him to his knees."

A friendly bank will call and tell you when you're overdrawn instead of crushing you by keeping it a secret. This will not really change the situation. It isn't as if you'll be able to run over there with a bale of money. But at least you'll be prepared for what's in store for you.

Banking by Mail. Never bank by mail. The tension involved in waiting to see if your money ever got there is one of the big contributors to cardiac trouble in America. Even if your name is Wodjikaciwizc, the bank will find *another* Wodjikaciwizc and return your bankbook to him.

Bank Etiquette. When you're standing in line at the bank, try to avoid peeking at the other person's deposit slip, to see if he's putting in more than you.

Bouncing Checks. Once checks start bouncing, there is almost no way to get them to stop, i.e., when the first one bounces, you can be sure that others will follow. The smartest thing is to get out of town for a while. Go to the Hamptons or Malibu for the weekend. When you get back, you'll feel more relaxed and better able to go over to the bank and start piecing through the rubble.

MONEY-SAVERS

A Subscription to *Mitten*. The quickest way for you to start saving is to cut down on the number of dirty magazines you buy. You should be able to get through on thirty a month. Try to zero in on your area of interest. If you're mainly interested in pictures of women wearing mittens, face up to it and stop kidding yourself. Take out a subscription to *Mitten* and hold it right there. Don't squander your money on magazines featuring non-mitten pictures.

Lonely Guys of the Future. Another sure-fire money-saver is to put all your loose change in a bottle and set it aside for a favorite nephew who is away at school. When he comes home for the holidays, *don't give him the money.* Keep it yourself. If you're too sweet a guy to go through with this, skim off the quarters and give him what's left. This same technique can be applied to trust funds for kids, those Lonely Guys of the Future, redeemable when they hit age twenty-one. Before that happens, start siphoning off the money, ostensibly for the kids' care, but actually to pay off the huge credit-card bills you must face up to.

Bargain-Hunting. Learn to think economically and to hunt for bargains. When veal is sky-high, pork-butts may be dirt cheap. By eating pork-butts every day for a couple of months, you can save a small fortune.

And don't forget off-season buying. The time to buy a heavy winter coat is not during the winter when you need it, but on the most sweltering day of the year when you can snap one up for a song. But be careful. Try it on quickly, and then whip it off quickly so you avoid heat prostration.

Things are always cheaper in some neighborhoods than in others. But don't buy any old thing just because it's cheap. What good will a hat-rack do you, if you've left your hat in Toronto? Even if it is cheap. The Lonely Guy who lugs home a giant bale of radishes often forgets that he will have to eat his way through them in order to justify this.

INSURANCE

By all means, take out insurance. Everyone has to do his bit to keep up this huge, wonderful industry that employs so many fine Americans. But never assume that you're actually going to collect on an insurance claim. The companies *say* they've paid off claims, but can you name a single fellow who has, as an example, lost all his suits and gotten paid back for them? Generally, the only ones who ever collect on insurance are drought victims.

An absolute must for the Lonely Guy is glove insurance. As a Lonely Guy, you probably lose around a half-dozen pairs a year, especially if you live in a chilly climate. Insurance companies, usually tough customers, are fairly softhearted when it comes to settling glove claims.

SAFE DEPOSIT BOXES

The One Big Danger. It's perfectly all right for you to sign up for a safe deposit box so long as you are aware of The One Big Danger. As the years roll along, you'll start imagining you've left all kinds of valuable items in there. This will set you up for a serious disappointment when you open it up and all you find is a skate key and some *Saturday Evening Posts*. Even worse, there may be some old sandwiches in there that you forgot about. So keep a safe deposit box, but don't start fooling yourself about what you've left in it.

Not Losing the Key. Make sure to keep the key in a safe place. Otherwise, the box will have to be blasted open. This costs more than you make on six months of unemployment.

TAXES

Fear of the Tax Man. Don't be afraid of the tax collector who, after all, is just a human being with the same doubts and inner fears that all of us have. Try to avoid direct contact with him, though, since if you meet face to face he will tend to know that you are lying through your teeth.

Get your accountant to tell the tax man that you are having a bit of a nervous disorder, which will always be more or less true.

If the tax man insists on seeing you in person, remember that the only way to deal with the government is to hurl a lot of paper at them. Fill a laundry bag with tickets, coupons, old *Playbills* from Broadway shows, veal piccata recipes, anything . . . dump it on the tax collector's desk and say: "It's all in there, fella."

Also, try to establish some common ground with the tax collector. Not something ridiculous. It's not important whether you both saw Ethel Merman in the original *Gypsy*. But maybe you both went to the same archery camp. Finding this out may not give you a tax advantage, but at least you will have come up with a talking point.

LAWYERS AND ACCOUNTANTS

Selecting a Lawyer. One of the secrets of business is to hire people who are good at it. This means taking on a crackerjack lawyer. Don't sign up with a huge law firm that has many partners and important clients such as the state of Oklahoma. Each time you visit your lawyer, he'll make you feel as though you're muscling in on Oklahoma's time. You are better off with a small scrappy guy who will yell and holler at people on your behalf, while you stay in the background being your charming self.

Paying the Lawyer. It's important to remember that lawyers charge for their time. So make sure you're calling about something important. Don't phone him to find out who he likes better, DeNiro or Pacino. Or because you're a little lonely. Make sure that you're at least calling to sue somebody. And no matter what the lawyer says, be sure to go ahead and sue because you're already deeply in debt to the lawyer as a result of calling him.

Selecting an Accountant. Most accountants will get infuriated when you eat in restaurants. They are pale fellows who don't have any fun and don't want you to have any either. They want you to live in one room and eat boiled potatoes. Get an accountant who doesn't mind if you eat out once in a while. Make sure your accountant is not afraid of the government. You don't need one who calls and says: "Jesus, they really got us now. I don't see how we're gonna squirm out of this one."

A good accountant will also lend you a couple of bucks when you're in a jam.

STATIONERY

Don't throw your money away on expensive stationery. Just rip off the ends of things, breadwrappers, telephone bills, other guys' letters, and use that. This will beef up your image as a modest Carl Sandburg type of fellow. Here is a sample of some perfectly acceptable Lonely Guy Stationery:

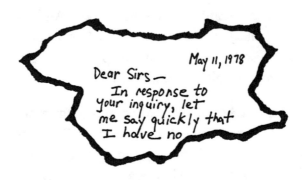

CREDIT RATINGS

Once you get a bad credit rating, it will follow you all your life and get passed on to your children, like hemophilia. The most amazing law on record says that credit companies are allowed to keep sending out bad reports on you for seven years after you've made your record spotless. If the credit companies had to keep their records up to date, it would require a lot of time and effort and get them all upset. No one wants to see this. So Congress passed this law to keep the credit companies from becoming cranky.

Only guys named Chip who live in Darien, Connecticut, have good credit ratings.

AN ACE IN THE HOLE

A Special Invitation. If you are under attack from a collection agent, you may have an Ace in the Hole you didn't know about. Instead of barricading your doors and hiding under the bed, invite the collection agent in to see your apartment. No agent in the world, no matter how hard-hearted, will be able to stand up to the sight of a Lonely Guy Apartment. A typical reaction will be: "Jesus, no one can live like this. I'm sorry I ever bothered you." The agent will then burst into tears and go away.

THE ACROSS-THE-RIVER DODGE

If you live in a high tax state, you can save a fortune by taking a small apartment across the river in a neighboring state where the taxes are lower. But you've actually got to live in that apartment. Dropping in once in a while to watch a little daytime TV will not appease the government. There are special teams of tax guys who run across-the-river bed-checks and won't give you a tax credit unless they see that your head touches the pillow every night and that you're fast asleep.

WILLS

Should You Make One Out. Lonely Guys often assume that making out a will is the same as dropping dead. This is absurd. It's just preparation.

Keeping It up to Date. Many Lonely Guys have dropped dead only to find they have accidentally left their money to the one who threw them out. So keep your will up to date. Find a Loved One, any old Loved One, and leave your money to that person.

The loneliest development in the world is when a Lonely Guy leaves his money to a highway.

Where to Do It. There is no reason for you to make out your will in a gloomy atmosphere. It doesn't have to be done in a crypt, with your attorney acting as Boris Karloff. The best place to draw up a will is in a cocktail lounge.

INVESTMENTS

Real Estate. The soundest investment continues to be real estate, which always goes up, until the time you want to sell it, at which point the market is generally "a little soft." The trick is to get rid of your real estate when you don't want to, when wild horses couldn't get you to part with it.

Never buy property in a country in which there is even a single insurgent up in the hills. Soon, mercenaries from Katanga will join him and they will all come down and get your land.

Dwarf Loopholes and Broadway. In the Sixties, many people got tremendous tax advantages by investing in dwarf ponies, but that loophole has now been plugged up. So have the dwarf date tree and dwarf turkey loopholes. All that dwarf stuff has been plugged up.

Under no circumstance should the Lonely Guy be talked into investing in or supporting the Arts. Even giving comfort to them is highly speculative. Unless he gets a crack at a hot Velasquez. Don't be talked into backing a Broadway show with the promise that you will get to sleep with the leading lady. One of the cardinal rules of show business is that the leading lady belongs to the director. If he insists, the investor will be allowed to watch the director sleep with her.

Stock Tips. The stock market is tricky. Many Lonely Guys bought stocks in the late Sixties on the assumption that the entire country, from Maine to Los Angeles, was going to be at leisure, every man and woman in the U.S. just bowling away the day. This never happened. Everyone is working harder than ever. If you had invested in work stuff—light bulbs, desks, coffeebreak wagons—you would be on easy street.

The best stock tips come from waiters in exclusive restaurants who get to overhear this kind of information while scraping up the breadcrumbs of important customers.

Try to sneak in and see movies before they open officially. If you really love the movie, and think it's going to be a blockbuster, run out and purchase the stock of the movie studio that made it. But make sure you're not the only one in the audience that loves it. If it's about giant man-eating boll weevils, and everyone else is snoring, you may be the only weevil man out there.

HIDDEN RESOURCE

Even though your back seems to be to the wall, you may not be as broke as you think. And no one is talking here about the potassium in your body after you keel over. Forget that. The phone company, for example, is probably holding a $25 deposit that technically belongs to you. You may own a life insurance policy that's worth another fifty bucks in cash. Throw in deposit bottles, Canadian coins you never bothered to cash in, Vegas casino chips, and little folded-up fives and tens in old windbreakers. It starts to add up.

The average Lonely Guy is worth around $185 more than he thinks he is.

RETIREMENT PLANS

As a Lonely Guy, you've been more or less retired all along. When it comes time for you to pack it in, how are you going to know? A more positive way to look at it is that a Retirement Plan is more essential to the Lonely Guy than to the everyday fellow. Most people are a little tired when they retire. Not the Lonely Guy. You've been saving up energy. When you hit sixty-five you really want to cut loose. So you should have a sound Retirement Plan, one that gives you as much cash as possible to throw around.

Lonely Guys, if they make it, are among the peppiest of old guys.

SUM-UP

While you sleep, an army of tax men, lawyers, accountants, agents and other assorted bad guys are out to get what little you have. If it's $1000, they not only want every dime of it, but they want a strict accounting of how you're going to get up the next $1000.

You can't win that war. No one can. In that sense, every American is just another Lonely Guy.

It will take all of your energies just to break even.

But you must not just keel over. Never simply hand over your money. At least do a lot of pissing and moaning and *then* hand it over. Let the sonsofbitches know they've been in a fight.

You may be an American Lonely Guy, *but you're also a man.*

Hats off to you and yours in your worthwhile struggle to become a financially solvent Lonely Guy.

ON THE COUCH

ON THE COUCH

As a child, he had a lovely singing voice but was quite shy about using it. He would consent to sing for company, but only if he could be under the piano. His sister would accompany him, and only when the song was completed would he come out from beneath the piano to take his bow.

At college, he agreed to be the M.C. for a variety show. Several hundred young women were in attendance, crossing and uncrossing their legs. He told a few jokes and then the microphone went dead and he could not silence the crowd. He fainted, and a hated economics major took over for him. When he was brought around, a fellow named Schapiro said: "I heard your jokes. They were terrific. What'd you have to faint for?"

He studied history under a professor who took the position that the Germans were not solely responsible for the start of World War One. One day, he was

119

chosen to debate this subject with some visiting students from Cambridge. They smoked pipes, wore shawls and seemed quite scholarly. He began with the statement: "The Germans were not solely responsible for the start of World War One."

"Indeed," said one of the Englishmen. "Why not?"

Suddenly, he forgot all the critical dates and codicils and Serbo-Croatian treaties he needed to support his argument. He was afraid of the fellow's shawl.

"Because they just weren't," he said and fainted.

When he recovered, he was told that a teammate had taken over and held the Englishmen to a tie, but that did not make him feel any better.

Can a psychiatrist help the Lonely Guy?

No reputable one will take him dancing or snuggle up to him on cold winter nights. But this option can give him something tangible to look forward to several times a week—a visit to the psychiatrist's office.

Many Lonely Guys have been frightened off by the public behavior of psychiatrists. Famed ones vomit routinely at dinner parties, pinching at hostesses and wrestling them to the ground. Others lose control of their sphincters at bond rallies and have to be led off in diapered disgrace. In spite of these shortcomings, a psychiatrist *can* be of aid to the Lonely Guy. One need only cite the example of Walter Alston, a hopelessly inept ballplayer who nonetheless coached the Brooklyn and Los Angeles Dodgers to immortality.

The decision to tie on with a psychiatrist should not be approached casually, the way one might stroll into a supermarket to check the new mustards. Psychiatry is only for those in urgent need of it. The best candidate for treatment may be the Lonely Guy who has no choice in the matter and is dragged in, feet first, foaming over with neuroses.

CHOOSING THE RIGHT MAN

Great care should be taken in the selection of a psychiatrist since both doctor and patient are in for a long haul. Treatment often drags on endlessly, until one of the participants falls by the wayside. If it is the psychiatrist, his wife may very well seize the reins and see the treatment through in the tradition of stalwart congressional widows. Should the Lonely Guy be the first to fall, his sons may want to leap onto the couch and wrap up their dads' complexes.

The Lonely Guy should take care to interview several doctors and not snap up the first to take an interest in him, as if he were at a Singles' Bar. One method of picking a psychiatrist is to think of someone who once behaved disgracefully—running up to strangers and head-butting them to the ground—and no longer does. The chances are that such a fellow has been taken in hand by a good psychiatrist. He may even *be* a good psychiatrist.

Though any old doctor can be of some help to the Lonely Guy, there is no reason to test this theory by signing on with a fellow who wears offensive suits or uses a whorish cologne. Obvious mismatches are to be avoided. The tall and shambling Lonely Guy will not flourish under the care of a short aggressive fellow who kicks at his shins to get his attention. Ultimately, the Lonely Guy must choose a psychiatrist whose style and manner he admires. No further thought should be given to the rejected ones, most of whom will recover in several months; worrying will not help them.

THE BARGAIN

A first meeting should be frank, with possible sticking points dissolved openly. Let's say the psychiatrist is an ex-Nazi. Rather than have this fact crop up later at some delicate point in the treatment—it should be put right out on the table. The ex-Nazi Lonely Guy should be equally forthright about his background.

The delicate matter of the doctor's fee is bound to come up at any first meeting. Some Lonely Guys, new to the couch, will be shocked and personally offended to learn that the doctor charges any fee at all, seeing this as one more example of moral decay in America. The fair-minded Lonely Guy, on the other hand, will agree that the psychiatrist has just as much right to loll about on Caribbean beaches as the next fellow.

The standard fee for treatment is in the neighborhood of $40–60 per fifty-minute hour. (The ten minutes between patients is designed to give the psychiatrist a chance to catch his breath, make a few calls and perhaps slap on a deodorant.) The Lonely Guy should beware of the doctor who charges some offbeat fee such as $37.50 per half-hour. Also suspect is the fellow who offers summer discounts and earlybird specials. On occasion, psychiatrists have been known to trim off a few dollars for the demonstrably needy patient. The Lonely Guy who benefits from a reduced fee should refrain from strutting about the waiting room and lording it over the other patients.

HOW TO BEHAVE IN THE OFFICE

Since the doctor will be watching him like a hawk, the Lonely Guy must be careful of his behavior in the psychiatrist's office where the most casual gesture takes on great significance. The Lonely Guy who kicks his feet up on the doctor's desk may be expressing some coquettish need to titillate the doctor with a Can-Can. A soft burp in the palm of the hand, innocuous in the workaday world, may represent an all-out attack on the doctor's values. The Lonely Guy who uses the psychiatrist's john in mid-session is taking his life in his hands. A single visit will lead to endless speculations about toilet training, especially if the doctor is from Vienna where great stock is placed in such matters.

A wise course for the Lonely Guy is to do as little as possible.

Early on, the Lonely Guy will have to decide just how much he wants to tell the doctor. There is no need, for example, to bring up the subject of his mom; he has a right to some privacy, after all. The same is true of sex; surely there is enough trouble in this world without getting down in the gutter. As a general rule, the Lonely Guy who tells the doctor too much risks losing his mystery and allure. No longer under his spell, the psychiatrist may turn his attention to other patients.

Theoretically, there is no boundary to what the patient can tell the psychiatrist, who is fond of saying that he is not a moral censor. Whether it be masturbatory practices on dogsleds or over-involvement with kneesox, the doctor has seen and heard it all. A word of caution, however. Even the most worldly-wise psychiatrist has his limits. The Lonely Guy who rambles on endlessly about his erotic interest in slime mold may eventually be shown to the door.

COUCH STRATEGIES

Normally, the psychiatrist will insist that the Lonely Guy lie down on the fabled couch. This is so that the doctor's presence does not become an interference, the Lonely Guy getting caught up in a distracting fantasy about his wrist hairs. There are several advantages to the use of the couch. Should the memory of a dead uncle cause the Lonely Guy to burst into tears, the psychiatrist—unless he rudely peers over—will not be able to witness this spectacle. Then, too, the couch can serve as a litmus paper of mental health. The Lonely Guy who clings to it and has to be pulled off at the end of sessions quite clearly has some distance to go in his cure. Conversely, the Lonely Guy who suddenly vaults off and refuses to spend another minute on it may be knocking at the door of self-confidence.

A disadvantage to the use of the couch is that it leaves the doctor unattended. There is no telling what he's up to back there. To rectify this situation, the nimble Lonely Guy, using the crook of his arm as a periscope, will be able to peer back and monitor his activities. Another technique is to catch the doctor's reflection in a shoe mirror.

As a general rule, no psychiatrist should be left unwatched for more than ten minutes at a time.

Most psychiatrists' couches will have lingering traces of perfume left by attractive young women who turned up for early sessions. There is no point in the Lonely Guy being shy about his interest in these. Quite boldly, he should ask the psychiatrist if it's all right to sniff some in.

HOW IT ALL WORKS

The basic style of the treatment is for the Lonely Guy to toss off story after aimless story until he stumbles across something of value. It is a great time-waster for the Lonely Guy to use up his fifty minutes on matters that are important to him, since they are never at the root of his difficulty. Only items that are preposterously insignificant are of the slightest bit of therepeutic use—he may as well get on with it and talk about them.

Under the psychiatrist's gentle guidance, the Lonely Guy will be steered toward a breakthrough— that is, a shaft of insight in which he sees that someone he always considered a loved one is a swine. Or that some swine is a loved one. The Lonely Guy himself may turn out to be a swine. Having arrived at this point, the Lonely Guy should be cautioned against leaping off the couch and organizing congratulatory benefits in his name. He should realize he's at about the same stage as the French who first broke ground on the Panama Canal. Only decades later did the first ship go sliding through.

If the Lonely Guy is unable to produce a breakthrough, the psychiatrist may show up one morning in a tutu, or posing as a Hartz Mountain transvestite, tapping at the underside of a breast and winking lasciviously at his patient. The Lonely Guy should see this tableau for what it is—a kind of psychiatric play-acting designed to jiggle forth the breakthrough from the repressed Lonely Guy. Only then should he decide if he wants to join the doctor beneath the couch.

THE IMPORTANCE OF DREAMING

Psychiatrists routinely use dreams as a centerpiece of treatment. Many Lonely Guys are under the impression that their dreams are brought in nightly from the West Coast, packaged by the same people who created "Roller Girls." When one is flimsy in plot, or an out-and-out turkey, their impulse is to call the coast and raise hell, like a Cable TV subscriber.

In reality, the Lonely Guy himself is the author of his dreams, responsible for gaps in storyline, lapses in taste and even dreadful acting. Not only does he write and direct his dreams, he also plays all the parts in them. If he dreams he is a seaman, adrift on the high seas with an ill-mannered Kurd, he is not only the seaman but the Kurd as well. There is only one exception to this rule: the horrifying dream in which the Lonely Guy is being chased by a sinister man. Examined closely, this awful fellow can be seen to be not the Lonely Guy but the psychiatrist, perhaps trying to collect his fees.

Dreams are essential to treatment and most therapists will insist that you have them. The Lonely Guy who has trouble in this area will be encouraged to eat chili peppers before turning in for the night.

FALSE MENTAL HEALTH

After a few sessions, the Lonely Guy will feel he is brimming over with mental health and may be tempted to dash through the streets with great goat cries of stability. This is a misleading time, similar to the "phony peace" that spread through Europe when Hitler conquered Poland and stopped momentarily to catch his breath. The psychiatrist has simply given the Lonely Guy a taste, a swatch, if you will, of well-being, of normalcy. The Lonely Guy may rest assured that in no time at all he will be plunged back into the gloom he has come to know and love, and that he will still need the psychiatrist.

WHO *IS* THAT OWLISH FELLOW, ANYWAY?

Ultimately, the Lonely Guy will wind up spending more time with the psychiatrist than he did with his mom. It is only natural for him to become curious about the fellow. What summer camp did he go to? Who are his friends? Is his wife a charmer? When asked about his personal life, the psychiatrist, depending upon his discipline, will either shrug or smile thinly.

The Unappeased Lonely Guy who spies on his doctor at night—or hires private eyes to follow him about—is in for a disappointment. For a psychiatrist, filling out a *Reader's Digest* sweepstakes blank is the height of rascality. Rare is the doctor who has been engaged to Liv Ullmann. On occasion, one will leap out of a high-rise, but most lead humdrum lives.

WHEN IT'S OVER

How can the Lonely Guy tell when his treatment is nearing the end? One theory is that it never quite does, and that Freud himself could have used a few brush-up sessions. Certainly, there is no official ending, a giant production number bringing the curtain down on *My Fair Lady*. Often, the treatment simply winds down, both doctor and Lonely Guy admitting they can no longer stand the strain.

It might be some chance event that tells the story, a stranger setting fire to the Lonely Guy's gym shorts. Previously, this action would have offended the Lonely Guy and thrown him off his game. Thanks to his years on the couch, he will see that there is little to be done about it and simply swat down the flames, smile patiently at the twists and turns of fate, and go about his business.

Psychiatry cannot banish loneliness. But it can firm it up a bit—perhaps enable the Lonely Guy to see clearly and unflinchingly for the first time what he is and what he may always be—a you-know-what.

AT THE
TYPEWRITER

AT THE TYPEWRITER

He wrote an essay in junior high school in which he used the phrase "Black clouds of Nazi oppression." The teacher took the position that no boy in junior high could make up such an expression. He was given a low grade and for the rest of the semester he was shunned as the boy who stole the phrase: "Black clouds of Nazi oppression."

As a Lonely Guy, you've got all that unhappiness and melancholy, just sitting there, going to waste. Why not cash in on it, using it for fun and profit? The way to do that is to become a writer.

You'll get to stare at people with blazing intensity and not be thought rude. You'll be able to sit alone over a drink, with bunched-up jaw muscles, as if life is too painful to contemplate; normally, this would be considered boring. Not if you're a writer.

If someone calls, and you don't feel like talking,

all you have to say is "I'm working." The caller will retreat in embarrassment and shame, convinced he has caught you in mid-Canto and thrown off your rhythm. Your erratic behavior will be excused. If you are at a party and suddenly sling a model over one shoulder, slipping the muenster cheese in your back pocket, someone will chuckle and say: "Don't mind him. He's one of those crazy writers."

You'll get to end love affairs abruptly, offering no explanation, and not be considered an ingrate. You're sensitive. You have your work. Even your crushed and rejected girlfriend will fly to your defense.

How does all that sound to you, Lonely Guy?

If it's your kind of madness, read on.

WHAT KIND OF WRITER SHOULD I BE?

Absurdist. The easiest kind of writer to be is an absurdist. All you've got to do is start jokes and not finish them. Have a character ask: "Is that a Sloth sitting next to you?" and don't let anyone answer. Let the question hang there, giving off echoes of Alienation and the Spiritual Impoverishment of Man. If you complete the joke, all you are is an amusing fellow. No critic will take you seriously.

Satirist. A satirist is a fellow who writes with a cool and veiled rage about the foibles of modern society. If you decide to be a satirist, make sure your rage is veiled. Calling someone a "no-good sonofabitch" is not good satire.

It is difficult to support a family on satire.

Ironist. An ironist is a fellow who can't sustain a good story. So he throws in a lot of stuff that doesn't fit. Twenty pages, out of nowhere, on axle grease. Anyone who objects to this long axle grease section has missed the irony.

It is impossible to support a family on irony.

Jewish-American Writer. All the fine Jewish writers insist that their writing is not Jewish. They are commenting on the *human* condition, not the Jewish one. They can't help it if it comes out sounding Jewish. This has created a need for a new Jewish writer who admits that his material is a little Jewish. Even if he is not Jewish.

WHAT SHOULD I WRITE ABOUT?

"Mel was depressed." A lot of notable writing comes out of unhappiness. This does not mean you should hack off a toe just to make sure you're miserable. Go with what you have. As a Lonely Guy, you should be set up nicely in this area. Remember, though, that unalloyed misery on the page is not necessarily rousing.

The line "Mel was depressed" at the beginning of a

book is no guarantee that the reader will fly through the pages to see if Mel ever gets to feel better. A few curiosity-seekers, perhaps, but not enough to send the book zooming up the lists. At minimum, have Mel feel depressed as he is diving beneath a Sardinian reef, where no man has ever felt depressed before.

A Trip to Kabul. Does travel help? Not necessarily. You don't have to go to Kabul to write about it. In fact, some of the best Kabul stuff has been written by guys who never went near the place. All they did in preparation was to read a few books about the area, written by fellows who'd never been there either. What they all came up with was Mythic Kabul, something no local Kabul man could ever approximate. Kabul critics eat that up.

Nothing to Say. How can I write a book? you might ask. I've got nothing to say. Don't let that stop you. Very few writers have anything to say. The trick is to see how long you can conceal that from the reader. The most successful writers are ones who've been able to get away with it for the greatest number of pages and years.

WHO SHOULD I WRITE FOR?

This is an age-old dilemma. Who is that fellow whose face I should be staring at as I write? Who will laugh at my jokes? If I write for someone smarter than I am, he'll see right through me. If I write for a dumb guy, I'll be writing a lot of dumb stuff. I can't write for myself. I'm on to all my old tricks. I'll put myself to sleep.

The best person to write for is Bianca Jagger.

WHERE SHOULD I BEGIN MY STORY?

All new writers agonize over this question. Should I begin with Glynis contemplating the new maturity of her body? Or Andrew caught up in the aroma of fresh muffins? The answer is that it doesn't matter. If your destination is downtown Vancouver, the important thing is to get there. Any road will do.

It helps, however, to make your beginning relevant. Why make life difficult by kicking off a War of the Roses yarn with a list of your favorite movie stars. Unless you're one of those fellows who fiddles around with traditional concepts of time and space. Remember, though, that Twentieth isn't really interested in those fellows.

TRICKS AND TOOLS OF THE TRADE

A Fascinating Typewriter. The kind of typewriter you choose will invariably influence your work. If you select a sturdy, high-backed type, you may find yourself taking on crusty, muckraking themes. Lashing out at the meat-packing industry and giving Lockheed a good tongue-lashing. A spare, cool-looking model that sends off a low impersonal hum will inevitably have you examining East-West themes, EuroComm and the complexities of modern industrial society. And you may not want to get into those areas.

So make sure you pick *your* kind of typewriter. And keep it fairly basic. The idea is to do fascinating work, not have a fascinating typewriter.

When You're Stuck. When you're stuck, switch over to a pencil. This will take you back to that time when you were a kid and writing was easy and natural and joyous. If this doesn't work, just be quiet when you're stuck and don't do anything for a while. Don't try to write your way out of it. No one wants to spend $12.95 for a book to see how the author tried to write his way out of something.

A Quiet Place. Do your writing in a quiet place. But not too quiet, or all you'll be able to write about is Alienation. This is not a good idea—unless Twentieth changes its mind and decides to get back into it.

Wide Margins. Use wide margins, not to cheat the publisher, but to give the reader a rest at the end of your sentences. A wide margin is like a pitstop to the weary reader.

Short or Long Sentences? Obviously, you've got to go with either short or long sentences. Short ones are good if you know what you're talking about. Otherwise, your ignorance will stand out. Long, run-on sentences were invented by writers who didn't know what they were getting at but figured they'd come up with something if they kept the sentence running on long enough, like the one you're reading.

Sights and Sounds and Smells. Try to recreate faithfully the sights and sounds and smells of everyday life. If you have trouble doing this, subtly smear a little marinara sauce at the bottom of the page.

FILM SALES

Every writer dreams of selling his book to the movies. There is no shame in that. But no serious writer ever lets this influence his work. Or decides ahead of time that he is after a film sale. If it works out, fine. If not, no problem. So the idea is to work on each sentence until you are satisfied that it serves the best interests of twentieth-century literature. Only then should it be scanned thoroughly to see if there is something for Redford in it.

THE FEMALE POINT OF VIEW

Many great writers have never mastered the knack of writing from the female point of view. Putting on a petticoat each time you come to the woman's part won't really do it. And you'll be exhausted from changing clothes all the time. The trick is to write the dialogue as if you are writing it for a male:

"Shut up, you worthless swine," said Derek.

139

Then switch over and attribute this same line of dialogue to a woman.

"Shut up, you worthless swine," said Susannah.

To cement the deal, you can do the following variation.

"Shut up, you worthless swine," said Susannah, prettily, with a whispered rustle of her petticoats.

You are writing from the female point of view. And no one will be able to guess your secret.

SEXY WRITING

Any moron can write about surging breasts and tumescent loins. The trick is to be subtle about it, to keep the sex out of view, but beating up against the surface. Make sure it's beating up there, however. Don't write a page about breadcrumbs and expect the reader to get all turned on.

CRITICS

No serious writer pays the least bit of attention to critics. He may stick his finger in one's eye every now and then. But that's the extent of his interest.

HELP FROM OTHER WRITERS

Other writers are the most generous of people when it comes to sharing their knowledge and craft. If you need encouragement, don't be shy about seeking out an established writer and asking him for help. The only time he'll clam up is when he senses you're about to get the picture.

THE HEMINGWAY LEGACY

Few writers contributed more to literature than Ernest Hemingway. But he also caused a lot of damage. The worst thing he did was to announce that he did his best writing at "first light." Ever since then, writers have been rolling out of bed at four in the morning, cranky and irritable, pecking away. Did anyone ever catch Hemingway working then? He was a competitive fellow and may very well have been trying to get other writers to work when they were exhausted.

A WRITER'S DAY

Here's the way to arrange your day as a writer. Forget "first light." Get up at a reasonable hour. It doesn't matter when—so long as you do get up. Eat a good breakfast, one that sticks to your ribs. As a writer, you need all the strength you can get. Read the newspapers and knock off around eleven or twelve magazines so that your work reflects the tenor of the times. Check the mail to see if anyone sent anything back. Smoke a cigar, which should get you a little drowsy. Drop off and get a little more sleep, since, as a writer, you need all the rest you can get.

When you wake up, eat a couple of nectarines to

get your motor going again. Hunt and peck a few sentences. Call up a friend and try them out on him. If he doesn't fall on the floor laughing, throw them out. Check the mail again, in case you missed a letter that was wedged in the corner of the mailbox. Make up a few more sentences, but don't try them out on your friend this time. Go to the delicatessen, order a tongue sandwich and see if you can pick up anything from the interesting characters who work behind the counter. So your work reflects the tenor of delicatessen life.

On your way home, stop at the Chinese laundry, in case some of your shirts came back early. Be on the alert for interesting stuff to write about in the laundry. Way in the back, where they eat, and all the interesting family stuff goes on.

When you get back, see if the toaster needs cleaning. If so, go to work on it. It's hard to write when you know there's an accumulation of eleven months' worth of English muffin crumbs in there. While you're digging them out, you can be working up ahead, on your writing. Try a few more sentences. If all you can come up with are one or two, don't be discouraged. Remember, they add up. At the end of the year, you may have forty or fifty, which will put you ahead of Beckett. Call up some friends to make sure they're not getting anything done either.

Go out and pick up a fish for dinner. Make sure its eyes are sparkly. When you get back home, watch the six o'clock news, so that your work reflects the tenor of television. After dinner, hang out at a bar that's filled with colorful characters. If you hear something colorful, run home and write it down so you don't forget it. Only frequent nearby bars, so you're not exhausted from running back and forth. Don't pick up any girls. As a writer, you need all the energy you can store.

Before you go to bed, read some other guy's successful book and try to keep your anger in check.

There you are. A Day in the Life of a Writer. Not much different from yours, is it? Except that you'll be putting That Sinking Feeling to constructive use.

So what are you waiting for? Don't just sit there and ruminate. Hit those keys. Take a shot at fame, fortune, trips to the Coast and an altogether new source of heartbreak and misery.

PART THREE
PERKS

THE LONELY GUY WISES UP

Finally, he saw what was wrong.

He was worrying too much about the wrong things.

He worried about Catfish Hunter's sore shoulder, Bill Walton's feet and whether Lyman Bostock could possibly play well enough to justify the 3.5 million the Angels had invested in him. He was still concerned about Willis Reed's knees. He worried about Sammy Davis' crushing schedule, Lorna Luft's apparent lack of a clear direction for her career and Cher's inability to find a meaningful relationship. McQueen's price concerned him and so did CBS's seeming inability to overtake pesky innovative ABC.

So one day he stopped worrying about these things and immediately he felt better.

All he had to do now was stop concerning himself with Carter's declining popularity and whether *Jaws 2* would outgross *Godfather I* and he would be in the clear.

THE LONELY GUY
AND HIS DOG

THE LONELY GUY
AND HIS DOG

*A dreadful fellow came to live in the neighborhood.
He was blond, well-muscled, and although he pre-
tended to be sixteen, the feeling was that he was
secretly older, possibly in his twenties. He had a
little white dog. He smashed younger boys against
playground walls and hurled fully grown war veterans to the pavement. He seemed totally evil. The
only thing that did not fit was the little white dog.*

For the Lonely Guy who can't get along with a person, a dog may be just the ticket. He can start with
a dog, see how it goes, and then shift over to a human
being. Or he can stop with the dog. It's up to him.

But a dog has its limitations. Finally, it's only a
dog. Just because it can run after a stick does not
mean that it can field questions on Turkish politics.
The Lonely Guy who yearns for a pretty and delightful young woman who works on a Drug Experimen-

tation program at Barnard College will not be satisfied with a dog. One of the reasons a Lonely Guy will hug and squeeze his dog so much is that he is unconsciously trying to turn it into a witty person. This cannot be done. A dog must be put in perspective. Otherwise, the Lonely Guy will wind up more confused than ever.

Here are some of the good things about a dog and some of the drawbacks.

GOOD THINGS ABOUT A DOG	DOG DRAWBACKS
A dog is affectionate.	There is no way to get a grip on a dog so that you can give it a legitimate hug. You wind up hugging it around some delicate reproductive organ. Also, a dog is limited in the way it can express affection. The Lonely Guy who requires a variety of techniques will soon grow weary of the same old unimaginative licks and snuzzles.
A dog smells great.	Puppies smell fine. Old dogs don't smell that terriffic. But when it comes to dogs in their middle period, it's not that

clearcut. One of the toughest and most exhausting things to figure out is if a middle-aged dog smells all right or if it's a little off.

You can always figure out a dog.

On occasion, a dog will get a strange lopsided look on its face. It isn't hungry. It isn't thirsty. It just looks weird. This look may go back to a time when the dog had to get up at the crack of dawn and run around in primeval packs. Or it may not. Perhaps the dog just realized that it's a dog, and doesn't know whether it likes it or not. You can go crazy trying to figure out that look. In the long run, you'll just have to give up.

A dog is easy to feed.

A dog is never finished eating. Anything it eats is considered an hors d'oeuvre. If it were up to the dog, it would eat until it became an elephant. The dog assumes that any food brought into the house belongs to the dog. A pastrami sandwich arrives, it's for the dog. The dog feels hurt and betrayed when anyone else eats something. No one has ever successfully explained to a dog that people need nourishment, too.

A dog is alert.

A dog may be too alert. A dog can tell when bad news is coming, long in advance. If it were not for the dog, a Lonely Guy could enjoy himself, right up to the arrival of the bad news. But the dog won't have it that way. The dog knows when the Lonely Guy has been rejected or turned down for something.

A dog even knows when there are parties going on that you haven't been invited to.

A dog is loyal to its master.

We assume that a dog is loyal to its master because of *Lassie*. But we don't know this for sure. Say you live in Apartment 14-H. One day, your dog accidentally wanders off the elevator into 10-H. The fellow there gives him unlimited Gainesburgers, and to clinch the deal, throws in Alpo Swedish meatballs, which are irresistible to a dog (and don't taste bad to a person, either). It's a harsh thought to contemplate, but the dog may decide to tie on with the guy in 10-H and never give you another thought. Even though you have slaved over the dog and played Fetch with him for fourteen years.

When you are dealing with a dog, there is always the lingering suspicion that if you're both trapped in a mineshaft for a week or so, the dog will start to eat your legs.

A dog will protect you from bad people.

A dog will protect you from wonderful people, too. It doesn't edit. If a person of the finest moral character shows up at your doorstep, the dog may behave as if the caller is Charles Manson, out on a work-release program. When great-looking women from Texas show up to collect for something, the dog may chase them away, too.

On the other hand, the dog may very well run right over and lick an embezzler.

A dog will attract women.

A dog will attract women to the dog. Not to you. These women are legitimately interested in the animal. They are not using this interest as a cheap ploy to get to meet you.

There is nothing lonelier than standing on the street with a collie that is surrounded by adoring women.

A dog will never scold you.

Sometimes you *should* be scolded. Say you did something rotten, refused a date with a distinguished anthropologist because she had fat ankles. The dog will act as if you just did volunteer work in a hospital. When Hitler marched into Poland, the first one to congratulate him was his dog. Shouldn't *Blondi* at least have bitten the Führer on the ankle?

A dog is easy to take care of	A dog would be easy to take care of if it were not for the decision-making. What exactly is a dog allowed to sniff at? How long should it be permitted to inhale building corner smells? If another dog bites your dog, should you encourage your dog to bite it back? Demand an apology from the owner? Hack at his neck? A great deal of mental strain goes into making these decisions.
A dog is easy to travel with. You just sit the dog up in the back of the car.	A dog sitting in the back of a car will remind you of a retarded niece in a Flannery O'Connor story who is being taken to a state institution.
Dogs have beautiful names.	Each time you call out the beautiful name..."Melissa"... "Heather"...it will remind you of the Melissa or Heather you are not allowed to have.

A dog allows you to feel superior.

Most dogs have better blood lines than their masters. If you step out of line, the dog will give you a haughty look, a reminder that its forebears yipped along at the heels of Louis Quinze. And that you are a fellow from the South Bronx.

If you own a dog, you no longer have to sleep alone.

Dogs are terrible sleepers. A leaf falling in the next county will have the dog leaping out of bed and howling out the window. No one can snore like a dog. If a dog has nightmares, forget about it. Anything can cause a dog to have a nightmare. It doesn't have to be important. It might be a little piece of meatball that got away and rolled under the refrigerator.

A dog will always take the most comfortable part of the bed, forcing the owner to sleep around the dog.

A dog will end your loneliness.

A dog may end your freedom, too. Once you commit to one,

you can't play with it and then hang it up in the closet like a London Fog raincoat. It's always *there,* staring at you and reminding you of something you didn't do for it.

The Lonely Guy should think long and hard before signing on a dog. A dog is a bit of a Lonely Guy itself. And two Lonely Guys do not add up to one happy fellow.

One approach is to test-own a dog, borrow one and take it away for a weekend. Or perhaps accept a visit from your ex-dog, with the clear understanding that if it doesn't work out, the dog gets shipped back to wherever the hell it came from and not a peep out of it.

If a Lonely Guy can accept a dog's limitations—and not keep blaming it because it isn't a gorgeous immunologist—he can find a small amount of happiness with the dog.

Whatever his decision, he should not let himself get talked into a goldfish.

HOW TO TAKE A
SUCCESSFUL NAP

HOW TO TAKE A SUCCESSFUL NAP

He dozed off during an Army training film and was brought before his commanding officer, a Dutch reservist who normally sold cars in St. Louis. "I don't want anyone in my squadron reported for schleeping, understood?"

"Yes, sir," he said. And then, mimicking the Major perfectly, so as not to be thought insubordinate, he said: "I'll never schleep again."

"Are you making fun of me?" asked the Major.

"No, sir," he said.

"All right then. And no more schleeping."

On rare occasions, and against all odds, a Lonely Guy will be spotted walking about with a cozy self-satisfied little grin. What is his secret? The chances are that he is a successful nap-taker.

The nap has traditionally been maligned as a destroyer of sleep. Let the Lonely Guy succumb to one and he will spend the night staring at the ceiling, eyes seething with activity. At its most diabolical, the Gestapo was unable to devise a more effective sleep-killer than the fifteen-minute snooze.

This is an unfair charge. Naps can lead to other naps. Experienced nap-takers can chain-nap their way along so that there is very little of the day to worry about. The nap can also serve as a drowsy little aperitif, whetting the appetite for a night of serious sleeping.

Not all men are gifted nap-takers. The secret of this art is doubtless one more piece of wisdom to be found scribbled away on the bulletin board of the all-knowing DNA cell. The average Lonely Guy cannot expect to make a sudden leap into World Class napping. By understanding the special nature of the nap, however, its whimsical ways, he *can* raise his proficiency and become a respected member of the napping community.

FIRST STAGE: TAKING THE NAP ON ITS OWN TERMS

The charm of the nap is that it cannot be planned with precision. Naps simply occur, unscheduled, unannounced, following a sleepy little drummer of their own. When a nap becomes possible, the untutored Lonely Guy will tear at his socks, hack away at tight underwear and may even issue a panicked call for an old childhood blanket. Before he can let out his first contented sigh, he will be more awake than ever—the frenzy of activity having made it impossible for the nap to take place.

In the same situation, the experienced nap-taker simply goes about his business—sharpening his scissors, polishing off a sonnet—pretending that nothing is up. He might be hooked over the arm of a chair or painting the bottom of a broom closet. No matter how uncomfortable his position, he will simply slump over and take his nap in peace, waving off the exaggerated dangers of circulation stoppage and possible amputation. In sum, the veteran nap-taker knows the fundamental napper's rule: Take the Nap on Its Own Terms. Do not try to re-schedule it for a more convenient time—or reshape it to other needs. That will come later.

There is one exception to this rule: In rare cases, a nap will come over him when the Lonely Guy is in an authentically slippery position—stretched out of a high-rise window, waving to a college friend, or in the outer lane of the Pacific Coast Highway, in a Chevy Nova. In such cases, quite obviously, the Lonely Guy must shift over to safer ground. But he must also take exquisite care to *stay inside the nap*. At this stage, the nap is like a plate of hot soup. Spill one drop and the Lonely Guy may well be up for seven days and nights.

SECOND STAGE: SECURING THE NAP

The second stage of nap-taking is hazardous precisely because it looks so easy. Once the nap has clicked in, the amateur tends to get cocky, rolling over with a happy yawn and assuming he is home free. The next thing he knows, he is sitting up in bed once again, saying: "Where did that sucker go?" This is because he has forgotten to Secure His Nap. The seasoned pro, on the other hand, grits his teeth, takes a firm hold on the reins, and in the only macho phase of nap-taking Shows the Nap Who's Taking It.

THIRD STAGE—DOWNHILL NAPPING

Once his nap has been secured, the experienced nap-taker is ready to settle in for some smooth sailing. To make sure there are no bumps along the way, he has done the following:

• Taken off his watch, one of the most important moves in nap-taking. A watch, during a nap, is ten times the bodyweight of the average Lonely Guy.

• Anchored himself down with a delicious snack, ideally a slab of pumpernickel with some cream soda so that the pumpernickel doesn't get lodged in there too firmly.

• Turned the radio to soft, innocuous music—so that he does not disco dance his way through the nap and wake up exhausted.

• Covered his feet, the most sensitive part of the

body during naps, not with socks, a blanket or other toe-cripplers, but with a light and gentle garment, an old windbreaker—or the flag of a small Latin-American country.

• Made a last-ditch sweep of his mouth, paying particular attention to lodged toothpicks and old forgotten macadamia nuts.

• Begun his nap in an awkward posture so that he can enjoy one of the napper's true delights—shifting over to his favorite position.

• Arranged himself so that he does not get couch button imprints on his back, which will have to be explained away.

Foot lightly on the brake, to avoid napping away an entire month, the Lonely Guy is ready to enjoy the most satisfying time of all—Downhill Napping, sought after by nappers the world over. Even at this pleasant juncture, however, the Lonely Guy is not quite out of the woods. Nappers never really are.

Here are some of the minor annoyances that might crop up and how to deal with them:

• Over-wide yawns which can lock in, yielding only to orthopedic skills. The napper must learn, reflexively, to smack himself when he feels one of these coming on.

• The phone. Arch-enemy of the nap. The Lonely Guy must decide quickly whether to answer it, or lie there twirling with indecision and killing off the nap. Established nappers have been known to carry on long conversations—and even make a grilled cheese sandwich—while still in the nap. The neophyte should not attempt this.

• Nap itches. The veteran napper, of course, scratches his in advance. Still and all, stubborn ones often slip by and should be handled with light, stroking, almost Zen-like motions, not clawed at with outrage. As for out-of-the-way shoulder-blade itches, the veteran napper prepares for these by keeping an object with an abrasive surface—such as a Brillo pad—in bed with him and backing his way up on it.

FINAL STAGE: MILKING THE NAP

Toward the end of Downhill Napping, the Lonely Guy will hear a faint and distant sound, similar to a conductor's voice: "Ronkonkama...everybody off for Ronkonkama..." This is a signal that the nap is nearing its end. While freshmen nappers make a mad dash for the exits, the veteran simply rolls over sleepily and prepares for the Napper's Endgame, known by aficionados to have its own special pleasures and rewards. The hard climb is over, the battle has been won. All he need do is dig his head a little deeper in the pillow and Milk His Nap, enjoying the napper's "second cup of coffee." In the darkest of all worlds, he will go past the station. However, in the napping community, this is hardly a disgrace and may even be overlooked with a rascally wink.

POST-NAP PERIOD

Once the nap has been accomplished and re-entry successfully carried off, the napper who is new to the game will turn his thoughts to mouthwash, planning dinner, taking his sleep-rumpled clothing to the dry-cleaners. Finally, he will begin to deal with the gnawing question that is so disruptive to all beginners: "How the hell do I get to sleep tonight?"

The professional napper—from his drowsy heights —will view all of this with amusement—and set about to do what every nap-taker worth his salt does: prepare himself for his next nap.

AT THE BEACH

AT THE BEACH

The father and mother were good at getting suntans. All they had to do was put their faces up to the city sun for a short while and they would get one. People would think they had just come back from a Caribbean island. They passed this gift on to their son who was fond of saying: "It's the finest inheritance a fellow could have." But secretly he wished they had left him a lot of money.

Every Lonely Guy needs fresh air, sunshine and a chance to get away from it all. The way to accomplish all that is to take an old-fashioned vacation at the beach. Some Lonely Guys who have tried the beach will scoff at the idea. They remember standing on the shore, staring at the horizon and getting a queasy feeling in their stomachs when they realized they were going to become part of The Great Beyond. The mistake they made was in assuming it was going

171

to happen that very minute. Sure, they would *eventually* have to join The Great Beyond. That's part of the package. But it might not happen until Labor Day. Or, who knows, maybe not for a season or two. Meanwhile, they should have relaxed and had fun at the beach.

The way to pull that off is to abide by a few guiding principles.

Forget about How Much It Costs. Beach vacations have inched up in price since you were a kid and now cost a fortune. Only emirs can handle them comfortably. The Lonely Guy who shells out all that money will feel a certain pressure to run around like a madman, trying to have fun every second of the day. Since there isn't a hell of a lot to do at the beach (the whole *idea* of the beach is there's nothing to do there) a conflict may arise, causing dizziness and vomiting. Now, what's the point of having to be flown back from an expensive vacation, a whipped and dejected man, as a result of worrying about all the money you spent on it. Aren't you better off putting the money out of your mind and getting sick about it later?

Go with the Body You Have. When the Lonely Guy finds out he is going to the beach, his first impulse will be to make a desperate last-ditch try for a new body, possibly by doing heavy squats in a nearby gym. This is ridiculous. By the time you make a dent in your fat, it will be September, time to go home. A better idea is to Go with the Body You Have. And go the limit with it, too. That means parading around in a bikini, putting your belly on proud display instead of hiding it in tentlike shorts. The first one to adopt this style on an international scale was the great film director, Roberto Rossellini, to the scornful amusement of Jewish mothers throughout the land, who said, "Look at that *pippick* (stomach)." Yet he won Ingrid Bergman, *pippick* and all.

Never Step on a Person's Dune. A dune is a beach person's most sacred and valued possession. It's what keeps his house and his children and the whole beach from floating out to sea and washing up in Macao. Rap a person's kids, needle him about his ethnic persuasion if you must, but stay away from his dune.

THE HOUSE YOU LIVE IN

"A Few Houses in from the Beach." ... The thing about a beach house is that it's either on the beach or it isn't. You don't get any points for being "just off the beach" or "a few houses in." The fellow who is "a short jog away" is in the same boat as someone who has to be brought in by Concorde. Neither one is *on the beach*. A fellow explaining how close to the beach he is is like a novelist telling everyone how much they love his book in England.

As a practical matter, make sure you are close

enough to the beach so that you actually get there once in a while. You don't want to be a Lonely Guy on the porch, questioning returning travelers about the beach. (Not that *stories* about the beach would be bad. What you would get then is the Myth of the Beach, which might be better than the beach itself, like Brecht's version of Alabama, a place he had never seen. But at these prices, you really should get a taste of the actual beach.)

The Hateful Security Deposit. Even houses that are far from the beach are terribly expensive because of the hateful Security Deposit, the worst thing in beach vacations. That's a huge sum of money paid to the homeowner in case you smash up his house. If you don't smash it up, you're supposed to get the money back, which, of course, is laughable.

Beach houses are specially made to look sturdy and rocklike upon examination and to fall apart at the touch the second you move in. Many were built by the same fellows who construct fake buildings for Hollywood sets. A sound policy is to kiss the Security Deposit goodbye, to consider it part of the rental fee and not spend the whole summer planning the fistfight you're going to have with the owner when he won't return your money.

Cleaning. Even though a beach house will collapse when you look at it too hard, it will be handed over in spotless condition, with a stern warning that it bettter be just as clean when it's handed back. Many Lonely Guys get sick about this and start cleaning the second they move in.

This is ridiculous. Even if you trucked in batteries of cleaning ladies and had them working round the clock, you would never get the house clean enough to suit the owner. His sole objective is to sock you with a "cleaning fee" and deduct it from your Security Deposit. So relax about this one, too. You're not out there to clean. Do you want to remember your vacation as The Summer of Cleaning? Of course not. Enjoy the beach, and on the day you leave, tidy up some and get the hell out of there as fast as possible.

The Bargain in Garbage Disposal. The only thing that's cheap at the beach is Garbage Disposal. It's as if all the beach people got together and said, "Let's keep the price down on one thing." And that's what they chose. So even if you're a Lonely Guy who only plans to have a little bit of garbage, sign up for Garbage Disposal anyway. Since there's so little to do at the beach, you may decide to join the crowd that drives out to the edge of town each week and heaves their garbage in the dump. Even if you become part of that group, save some of your guck for Garbage Disposal so that you can take advantage of the low price.

BEACH PEOPLE

The Owners of the House. During the summer, you may get the uneasy feeling that someone is spying on you. It might be a mysterious car, cruising by at dusk, the driver craning his head unnaturally. Or a strange couple, peering at you from over a dune. This is not your imagination out of control, an effect of TV crime-show saturation. Someone *is* spying at you, the owners, trying to find out what you've done to their house. By mid-season, they won't be able to stand it any longer and will knock on your door, under the pretense that they were just in the neighborhood and wanted to see if you figured out how to work the dryer. Don't fall for this ploy. They are lying through their teeth. Invite them in for just one piña colada and you'll have an all-out war on your hands when they spot bacon grease on a slipcover. At the end of the summer, make sure you're safely on the highway before the owners take over the house. No law says you have to stand by with bowed head and be scolded for accidentally mangling a saltshaker.

Houseguests: Beware of Liv Ullmann. You'll be amazed at how easy it is to get houseguests to come out to the beach. As an experiment, call up the president of Gulf & Western, invite him out and watch him take the next private plane. Why shouldn't he? The house is costing you a small fortune and all he has to do is show up with a bottle of wine. So sort out your guests carefully. If Liv Ullmann shows up for the weekend, make sure it's *you* she admires, not the weekend. When you get back to the city, you don't want Liv dropping you like a hot potato.

Singles. Every weekend, a whole bunch of Singles will turn up at the beach. The way to get close to an attractive one is to strike up a conversation about how wonderful the beach used to be until all the Singles discovered it. Unfailingly, she will agree with you and think that you're charming, extricating herself from the other Singles.

Year-Rounders. Many Lonely Guys assume that locals, or year-rounders, are surly, resentful of summer vacationers and only tolerate them so that they can get at their money. This is a harsh attitude. Thanks to television and such social visionaries as Norman Lear, the whole country is now one big community. Rural America has seen such shows as *The Jeffersons,* too, which has taught the locals that *all* Americans have the same hopes and fears as they do. As a result, rural folks can be counted on to wait until the last summer vacationer has departed before staging their Klan rallies.

One of the toughest romances to bring off is one with a local girl.

LONELY GUY: Can't we go out? This isn't
Ulster, you know.

LOCAL GIRL: We're from two different worlds.
There would be opposition from my parents,
my relatives, my colleagues at the frozen yogurt store.

LONELY: What if we met in the city?

LOCAL GIRL: Solid.

THINGS TO DO AT THE BEACH

Eating and Drinking. The great thing about beach
eating is that everything tastes delicious out there.
An old piece of celery you would sneer at in the
city becomes an irresistible taste treat. A simple hot
dog with mustard will have you rolling around on
the floor in ecstasy. Before the day has gotten under
way, Lonely Guys with frail appetites have been
known to inhale half a dozen eggs and a box of
sausages.

The best part about beach eating is that it will not
make you as fat a guy as it would in the city. The
same is true of drinking. The beach is an excellent
time to try out all those off-trail drinks you wouldn't
normally fool with—pear brandy, schlivovitz, Main-
land China Vodka, that kind of thing, none of which
will make you as nauseous the next morning as they
would in the city, either.

Some Cautionary Notes on Beach Eating: A thing to
watch out for is sand. The Lonely Guy will spot some

on a tomato and say, "Oh, what the hell, a little sand won't hurt me" and wolf down the sandy tomato. At the end of the summer, he's got a whole dune in his stomach, which won't come out that easily. . . .

Watch out for beach restaurants, especially ones offering gourmet meals, a contradiction in terms. Beach restaurants are notoriously inconsistent; they'll hit the heights with baked clams and send you roaring off in an ambulance with the roast beef. If you must go to one, order a grilled cheese sandwich, something they can pull off, and hold the line right there. Try not to get hungry for Chinese food, since the nearest Chinese restaurant is three hours away. If you know of someone who is driving out from the city, have that person save up the little white containers of leftover subgum and won ton soup from his last Chinese restaurant dinner and bring them out to the beach.

Don't get mad at bacon. There's something about the hot weather that gets people mad at it, for looking so nice in the package and then shriveling up to nothing. Bacon is bacon. It never claimed to be anything else. Try to enjoy it for what it is. . . .

Beach Movies. The beach is a great place to catch up on movies you wouldn't be caught dead seeing in the city. Films that are paralyzingly witless can be fun at the beach where you can hoot and holler at them to your heart's content. Many beach movie houses are fun in themselves, a bunch of chairs strewn about in an abandoned post office, giving you the feeling you're at a secret F.A.L.N. meeting. The two finest beach movies ever made are *Wrath of the Gods* starring Robert Mitchum and *Light at the Edge of the World* with Kirk Douglas and Yul Brynner.

Coming Up with a Philosophy. Most Lonely Guys scratch along from day to day and never give a thought to the Big Picture. They don't have a Guiding Philosophy to sustain them in their hour of need, which is every hour. The beach is an excellent setting for kicking around a few guiding philosophies and perhaps coming up with a winner. The best place to do this is at the edge of the sea. If you come up with one on a porch, it will be one of those Will Rogers crackerbarrel philosophies that won't stand up under real stress.

Once you're at the ocean, with the water lapping up against your shorts, you'll see clearly that all man's posturing and worrying is ridiculous since we're all just particles. That goes for everyone, from the most humble Chinese guy all the way up to Valerie Giscard D'Estaing, who, in the overall picture, is just another French particle. All particles eventually get shoved into the Eternal Stream, French ones, Hungarian particles, all of them. So isn't it ridiculous to worry about whether to put mustard or mayonnaise on a tongue sandwich, when we're all going into that stream?

In any event, that type of thinking, sharpened up a bit naturally, can stand as a philosophy. Trying to shape up a philosophy is a worthwhile activity, but take it easy when it comes to questioning the nature of reality. If you break through in that area, and prove, for example, that you're a prune danish, and not an accountant, you'll be resentful about all the money you're spending on this vacation.

Volleyball. From a distance, this game appears to be a happy-go-lucky affair; in actuality, it is one of the most savage and crippling sports known to Western man. Houses have had to be sold, tight families have broken up, ad salesmen have torn down nets and walked into the sea—all because of volleyball arguments and slights. Fellows in rest homes stare at walls aimlessly because they were once chosen last on volleyball teams, or not chosen at all. Volleyball is a perfect game for the Lonely Guy who wants to cut his last civilized ties with his fellow man.

Most beach volleyball games have been going on for fifteen years and are impossible for a newcomer to break into, the slots being passed along from father to son, like the stagehands' union. Your best chance to get into a game is to be on the sidelines when someone breaks a hip. But even when a newcomer gets into the game, he is still not in it since no one will pass the ball to him and for the first six summers he'll just stand there in isolation, the man in the iron mask.

Most volleyball arguments break out over whether someone has hit the net with his body, which is illegal; competition is so fierce that fellows accused of hitting the net have been taken to nearby laboratories to see if there are net strands on them. The basic unit in volleyball is made up of the "setter" and the "spiker," the former gently and lovingly lofting the ball up in the air so that the spiker can ram it down an opposing player's throat, ideally causing a disabling injury. The best way to earn a permanent place on the team is to become setter to a tall, ferocious spiker. This is very much like becoming the "girlfriend" of a tough fellow in prison who will see to it that no harm comes to you.

Getting Sick. The beach is not a bad place to be sick since beach doctors are surprisingly effective on anything up to a sore throat and will often bring off a cure where some lazy city doctor won't. The best thing about a beach doctor is that he isn't attending the Stuttgart Ballet, and you can actually get to see *him,* not his assistant. Beach drug stores are far ahead of the rest of the country when it comes to hay fever decongestants and the latest athlete's foot creams.

Worrying about Ants. Many Lonely Guys spend their entire vacation trying to figure out ant behavior. This is ridiculous since even the ants don't know what they are doing. Sometimes they come running out because a baked apple has been left uncovered. Other times, when all the food is wrapped up and in the refrigerator, they'll run out anyway and try to eat a bestseller. Ant intelligence has been over-rated. They are not that smart. The individual ant has a tiny and unspectacular brain, even for an ant. It's only when a lot of ants get together and pool their individual routine brains that they become smart enough to carry someone off. Don't waste your time trying to dope out the ant's every move.

The beach is an excellent place for the Lonely Guy to go on vacation provided he lowers his sights and doesn't expect to have too much fun. He can have a little fun. Also, it's not a good idea to go out there every year; nothing marks the passage of time more dramatically than an annual visit to the beach, each summer another ring around the Lonely Guy's neck. It's better to turn up every five or six years and have the Passage of Time thrown in your face in one big gulp. For his other vacations, the Lonely Guy should go elsewhere, up North where he'll be too cold to worry about time passing—or to the Mediterranean, where it's the passage of French time and doesn't count in the same way.

SEX AND THE
LONELY GUY

SEX AND THE LONELY GUY

As childhood cousins, they played "Doctor," but, as the saying goes, they went no further. She had wet, smouldering eyes, and a Forties' movie-star face. He lost track of her. Thirty years later, she showed up— at a time when he was having a puzzling but rich affair with a Chinese woman. He took his cousin to dinner and they went back to his apartment. Eyeing his bedroom, she said, "All these years . . . it's still the same."

"I'm sorry," he said, "but I can't handle a cousin and a Chinese woman at the same time."

Just because you're a Lonely Guy, it does not mean you've said goodbye to sex. Not by a long shot. There's tons of it out there, and it's your obligation to go out and scoop up some of it.

You're probably more interested in women than ever, the only question being how to proceed with them.

Men and women in the late Seventies don't have
the slightest inkling of what to do with one another.
Each sex looks at the other with a baleful eye. The
slightest gesture, scratching an ear, or the most inno-
cent question—"How are your tomatoes?"—is often
misinterpreted as a hostile act. New translators may
be needed between the sexes. Now that women are
equal, they feel a bit awkward about it and wonder
if they should have pushed so hard. Men would like
to reach out and help but are afraid they will be
smashed in the head. All men and women are miserable about this state of affairs, with the possible
exception of Fritz Mondale. Exhausted, battle-weary,
women have gone off to take walks in the Poconos
with their new friends—other women. Men sit alone
in the dark and watch dart competitions.

Into this grim arena steps you, the Lonely Guy.
What chance do you have for success with women?
Considering your past record, you may feel the question is absurd. But is it, really! Though you tend to
be a bit pale and green around the gills, you still
retain a battered charm. You know failure. Rejection
has been your friend. You are solidly grounded in
ineptitude. Tired of being misunderstood, you've
elected to be silent. This gives you the appearance
of being a wonderful listener. These qualities will
appeal to the discerning woman who does not reject
you on sight.

This is not to say that lovely young women will be

readily available to you. There is an abundance of them, but they are not all that easy to get at. In many cases, you will have to content yourself with seeing them pass in review beneath your windowsill, or disappear, heartbreakingly, into the arms of a Chilean. But you must continue to make a stab at getting some, no matter how thankless a task it seems. It's not essential that you succeed. Repeated tries will keep you in trim for that far-off day when you become A Lonely Guy No More.

What follows are guidelines for you, the Lonely Guy, in your bid for a slice of the sexual and romantic pie. If none seem applicable, remember that the greatest minds in history have fished in these very waters and rarely come up with a nibble.

A BASIC PHILOSOPHY

Despite a scar or two picked up in the recent Great Struggles, women are more appealing than ever, warm, sensitive, caring, almost absurdly in touch with your feelings and theirs, able to spot a nuance at a hundred yards, an emotional tremor at a thousand—and more confident than ever about throwing these attractive features into play. Since this is true of *all* women, you might just as well try to get yourself a gorgeous one.

CATEGORIES OF WOMEN

Jewish Women. The big news is The Return of the Jewish Woman, or Jewish-American Princess, as it were. Many have been to Tibet. Others faithfully attend Masturbation Class. A lot of them kiss back. Some are enjoying rebellious second marriages to narcotics cops and reportedly do not snap and pick at them, demanding, for example, that they better their arrest records. The Jewish Woman is still a little tough, but it is a new kind of gentle and giving toughness. Don't write off the Jewish Woman. There is no need to run out and buy her a Mercedes—but give her an even chance.

Famous Women. Just because a woman is famous and successful is no reason to give up on her. We have all heard the stories. Candice Bergen sits home on Saturday nights. Cybill Shepherd, same thing. So when Saturday night comes around, call up Candice Bergen. The chances are you will catch her as she is about to go out—because all those stories are ridiculous—but at least you will have the thrill of having made contact with Candice Bergen and not having spent a Totally Lonely Saturday Night.

Much Younger Women. Don't be intimidated by Much Younger Women. Considerable nonsense has been written about the pitfalls of such relationships —the Middle-Aged Lonely Guy and the Much

Younger Lovely Young Thing. There is only one real danger—younger women love to let out blood-curdling screams, leap out from behind couches and pretend their heads have been chopped off. As a fun thing. They can't, for the life of them, grasp why you may find this offputting. If you can surmount this one obstacle, it's full speed ahead on women many years your junior.

Less-Than-Great Beauties. At a certain point, you may decide that you have had it with beautiful faces and bodies, that all of this is fleeting and transient and that only sound character is of importance. Once you come to this realization, and you *still* can't get anyone to go out with you, then you are really in bad shape. You must tread lightly at this juncture.

Actresses. No one can be more charming if you have a part for them.

Models. Good, when they hit age twenty-nine and realize they are not going to get away with their behavior forever.

STRATEGY AND TACTICS

Picking Up Women. Many Lonely Guys have reported great success in picking up women. Literally picking them up, right off the ground. This tactic has merit if it is not applied indiscriminately. It would not be wise, for example, to race over and pick up Lillian Hellman.

Horniness. Just because you don't feel particularly horny on a given occasion, there is no reason to stay home and sulk. On the contrary, go out of your way to schedule dates on Nights When You Are Not Horny. Women will appreciate this. "What a pleasure," your date will say, "not to have to be mauled and pawed at for a change." This relaxed atmosphere will tend to make her horny after a bit. And there is no rule that says you can't become Suddenly Horny, too.

Standing Pat. Many a Lonely Guy fails at romance because he is constantly trying to improve his hand. With a perfectly acceptable woman in tow, he will peer about at parties and Singles' Bars for someone Slightly More Delicious, and wind up going home alone. A good rule is to snap up the first person who pays the slightest bit of attention to you. In nine cases out of ten, it will turn out to be the best you could have done.

Be Yourself. Learn to be yourself around women. As a Lonely Guy, you may feel it's a bit risky, but it must be done, nonetheless. If you read *Hustler*, don't hide the latest issue in the breadbox just because a woman is on the way. This approach can be overdone, however. There is no reason to leave heavy leather-bound volumes of *Enema Island* on display, just to show you have nothing to conceal.

Possessiveness. Never be possessive. If a female friend lets on that she is going out with another man, be kind and understanding. If she says she would like to go out with all of the Pittsburgh Steelers, including the coaching staff, the same rule applies. Tell her: "Kath, you just go right ahead and do what you feel is right." Unless you actually care for her, in which case you must see to it that she has no male contact whatsoever.

Taking a Shot. When you spot a lovely woman standing on a post office line or leaving Bloomingdale's, your normal impulse will be to think: "Oh, if she could only be mine," and leave it at that. Every now and then, it's wise to Take a Shot. Fall upon her with a great whoop and a goatcry and tell her how delicious she is and how anxious you are to take her to a restaurant. In almost every case, she will turn out to be living with someone, and desperately happy about it, but even this experience will not be wasted. Consider your little sallying forth as part of a series of practice rounds.

A Code of Honor. Never approach a friend's girlfriend or wife with mischief as your goal. There are just too many women in the world to justify that sort of dishonorable behavior. Unless she's *really* attractive.

A Weekend Game Plan. The worst dating time for the Lonely Guy is the weekend when the chances are he won't have one. An effective strategy is to schedule periodontal work on a Friday afternoon. This will keep you desperately uncomfortable until late Saturday night. At that point, you can say to yourself: "No sense calling anyone now. I might as well get the Sunday papers and pack it in." Simple as that, you'll be out of the woods. And you'll have tough gums, too.

Take a Meeting with Mom. Even in the New Culture, it remains true that the best way to tell how a woman is going to turn out is to meet her mom. So insist on Taking a Meeting with Mom. Your girlfriend may be the fairest flower beneath the sun, but if her mom looks like a utility infielder for the Montreal Expos, rest assured that your girl will eventually take on that Expo look.

A Most Desirable Relationship. Try to strike up a relationship with an ex-lover. The storm is over. Sex is out of the way. You can now relax, be friends, enjoy each other as people. Of course, these are terribly stimulating conditions, and you must be careful not to hop into bed again, in which case the whole business will become absurd.

NEW BEDROOM HORIZONS

The New Erogenous Zones. One of the great break-throughs in sex has been the discovery of all the new erogenous zones. Once it was thought there were only a handful. Now they are all over the place with new ones being reported every day. Don't try to go at too many at once. If you do, they will cancel one another out, with some of the traditional old-line ones being neutralized. A sensitive partner can help by tapping you on the shoulder and saying, "You are tackling too many erogenous zones."

Some of the newer ones are not immediately erogenous and must be cultivated a bit. It won't do to run over and start licking a knuckle, expecting erotic wonders. Later in the game, when the proper ground-work has been laid, that same laggard knuckle may suddenly turn tempestuous.

Dirty Talk. Women now freely concede that dirty talk is stimulating. Take this hint and start whispering a lot of it in your partner's ear. But make sure it's dirty. Halfway measures may backfire. For example, the line, "I've always had great admiration for your labia minora" might very well backfire, with chilling consequences.

Orgasm-Spotting. There is no question that women love to have orgasms. But many women are confused as to whether they have been able to pull them off.

You can be a good friend by helping to spot them as they turn up, hollering: "There's one right there" when a likely one is on the horizon. If your partner remains unconvinced, do not lose your temper and shout: "Goddammit, I know an orgasm when I see one." A much better tactic is to return patiently to the helm, and wait for a surefire one to loom into view.

In the case of some women, orgasms take quite a bit of time. Before signing on with such a partner, make sure you are willing to lay aside, say, the month of June, with sandwiches having to be brought in. It may be that you will prefer a partner with a quicker trigger, as it were.

The orgasm, finally, is a private experience. While one is in process, do not cry out, "Hey, what about me" and try to shoulder your way in on it. Though the experience may be a bit lonely, wait on the sidelines for it to blow over, at which time your patience will no doubt be rewarded and you will be ushered back onto the field.

S & M. As a Lonely Guy, you are probably familiar with lower back pain, and a host of other ailments. You may very well be a bleeder. Before joining in on the chic new S & M craze, make sure you sincerely want to spend an evening with a row of clothespins attached to your hips. You may decide in favor of a less elaborate alternative.

Surprises. Creativity is fine in sex. But try to avoid surprises. Unless you have announced it far in advance, do not suddenly reach over and pour a Boysenberry sundae over your partner's feet.

Generally, it is a good idea to keep sex simple. If equipment has to be used, make sure it is bundled up in advance and kept alongside the bed. Nothing is more disturbing than to have to call things to a halt while you rummage through old cartons for a Pinocchio costume.

Role-Changing. No longer is there a stigma attached to changing roles in sex. If you feel a wave of femininity coming on, you can now safely lie back and enjoy it with no fear of losing your job in the State Department. But once having switched over, remember to switch back. Many Lonely Guys have made the switch and never been heard from again. It may be that you will want to set the alarm. The ringing of the bell will be jarring, but it will remind you to get back on that original road.

Three-Way Sex. The New Woman will very often, happily and lovingly, invite her girlfriend along for you to enjoy. All three of you will be expected to tumble into bed and there is no question that the experience will be tasty. But watch for the catch. The following weekend, you may be expected to haul out another male, so that your girlfriend can have a shot at him as well. Before embarking on three-way sex, be sure you are willing to make room in your bed for Roosevelt Grier.

Foreplay. Everyone loves Foreplay, and you, as a Lonely Guy, should not avoid it. But don't get hung up on this activity, either. Eggrolls and spareribs are delicious, but they are not an end in themselves. At a certain point, it becomes time to push on to the Sliced Prawns with Black Bean and Garlic Sauce.

Positions. There is much to be said for the basic positions. The top one has a Conquering Hero flavor, just as being on the bottom brings along with it a certain Ghandi-like Strength. As a Lonely Guy, your best bet may be Sideways. When you are ready to call it a day, you will not be as tempted to leap off, gasping for air. All you need do is remain where you are and sink down for a quick chat, followed by a catnap. Added to this, Lonely Guys look their best from the side.

Final Word on the Clitoris. Once and for all, there *is* a clitoris. For a while, in the early Seventies, a theory took hold that it did not exist—that it was to be put in the category of Flying Saucers, with occasional sightings, none of them verifiable. Beyond the shadow of doubt, its presence has now been established, although it does tend to wander off now and then. In any case, the Lonely Guy must prepare himself to be on the lookout.

The Bonus. There will be times when you may not feel terribly sexy. "How can I be tumescent," you ask yourself, "when I'm a little down?" On those occasions, think of the middle linebacker who plays while in pain. The novelist who uses his gray periods to rip off bestsellers. The downcast actor who flies in from the wings.

And there's a bonus—your wailing sounds will be taken for passionate ones. An agonized teeth-gnashing grimace will slip by as a look of ecstasy. Cry out: "I can't take it any more." Your partner will assume you're finding it all unbearably delightful.

Sex is too important to be sloughed off. Never before has so much of it been available to so many, including the undeserving.

It is your responsibility, as a Lonely Guy, and as an American, to go out and get some before it all goes away.

EPILOGUE
WHITHER THE LONELY GUY

He pictured himself, in years to come, sitting each day on the patio of the Gritti Palace in Venice and staring at the Canal. When tourists asked about him, the padrone would say: "He is the American. They say he once wrote very well and had extended correspondence with Alfred Kazin. He does not write any more. He arrives here each day, orders a Negroni and waits for the Contessa who will not come."

As a Lonely Guy, you can expect to wake up one morning with a nagging lack of anxiety. Step outside and you will notice a discomforting bounce to your step. To compound the state of affairs, you will probably have a sense that all is right with the world.

Don't be alarmed. All Lonely Guys go through this experience. It is known as "free-floating happiness." It probably won't last.

Be patient. The chances are that before long that

Comfortable Sinking Feeling will soon return. And you'll be back at the old post, leaning over railings, listening for the sound of foghorns, staring off in the distance and steeling yourself for the next off-trail development in your life.

No one, finally, can strip you of your loneliness. Into the world you came as a Lonely Guy. Out you will go, withered, a bit wiser, but pretty much in the same state. Loneliness is a natural condition of life, as anyone who has ever looked at a forlorn and bewildered amoeba under a microscope can testify. Few, if any, make it to the Other Side. Most are eventually driven back, like Norse invaders.

Isn't it possible, then, in some way, to stop dead on a dime and become A Lonely Guy No More?

Sometimes life itself will lend a hand.

> LONELY GUY (opening door): Jeremy! What are you doing here?
>
> EX-SON (carrying a suitcase): Hi, dad. I heard you were lonely. I'd like to spend my last year with you before going off to Furman U.
>
> LONELY GUY: This is an awfully small place.
>
> EX-SON (entering): Don't worry about it. You'll hardly even notice me. Where do I put my collection of *Iggie and the Stooges* records?

Or else:

> LONELY GUY (opening door): Diana! What are you doing here?

> LOVELY REGISTERED NURSE (who altruistically ministers to the sick and the lame): I'm moving in. Don't try to stop me. I love you and I'm going to make you happy if it kills you.

Barring some such dramatic turn of events, most Lonely Guys will have to pick their way through life on a day-to-day basis, taking whatever cards life has dealt them and trying to bluff their way to happiness.

Don't fritter away badly needed energy in an attempt to change your nature. You're a Lonely Guy! Get comfortable with your loneliness. Whether you stay home with it, take it out sailing or hold it aloft like a banner at the Cannes Film Festival—enjoy it. Years later, you'll want to look back on your Lonely Guy days as a rich and fascinating time of your life, like the Army.

> HOUSEFUL OF GRANDCHILDREN: Tell us what it was like when you were a Lonely Guy.
> EX-LONELY GUY (now an Advanced Adult— with a sly smile): It wasn't bad. Not bad at all.

Bacon cheeseburgers, Cheryl Ladd posters, Ibsen revivals, pine tar room fresheners, the scent of wisteria on another guy's terrace—they're all out there for the Lonely Guy with red blood in his veins and the courage to say: "I can have these things, too, even though I happen to be living alone for the moment."

Hats off and a fond farewell to you, Lonely Guy, as you hunch those shoulders squarely, swallow hard, hang your head medium-high—and valiantly set forth in pursuit of your small but very own quite legitimate share of the pie.